Another Taste Of Washington State

A Recipe Collection
From
The Washington State
Bed & Breakfast Guild

Edited by
Tracy & Phyllis Winters

Winters Publishing
P.O. Box 501
Greensburg, Indiana   47240

800-457-3230
812-663-4948

Front cover photograph: By Robert Montgomery
View from Hillside House Bed & Breakfast
Friday Harbor, WA

Back cover photographs: Sunset view from Soundview Bed & Breakfast
Seattle, WA
Valley view from Stratford Manor Bed & Breakfast
Bellingham, WA

Divider page calligraphy by Mary Rose Hawkins

Divider page art by Melissa Pigg

The directory information about the inns and the recipes were supplied by the
inns themselves. Every effort has been made to assure that the book is accurate.
Neither the editors, The Washington Bed & Breakfast Guild, the individual inns
nor the publisher assume responsibility for any errors, whether typographical
or otherwise.

Library of Congress Card Catalog Number 00-106797
ISBN 1-883651-15-8

Preface

The Washington State Innkeepers welcome you to a Bed & Breakfast experience in the Northwest's breathtakingly beautiful Evergreen State. Enjoy a diversity in lodging as you travel to participating member inns. Each inn reflects its innkeeper's individual expression of warm hospitality, comfort and caring for your needs, plus of course, delicious breakfasts! We have storybook Victorian, historic and colonial homes, mountain lodges, log inns, contemporary homes, beach houses, country homes and farmhouses, to private cottages and executive suites.

The Washington Bed & Breakfast Guild is an association of Washington State inns. Its Board of experienced innkeepers has established membership criteria, while dedicating itself to preserving very strict standards of quality for its members. Each member inn is LICENSED, INSPECTED and APPROVED and must operate at or above these high standards of quality for continued membership.

A complete directory of all members of the Washington Bed & Breakfast Guild can be obtained by request to the following address or toll-free phone number:

Washington Bed & Breakfast Guild
2442 N. W. Market Street, #355
Seattle, Washington 98107

1-800-647-2918
www.wbbg.com

Dedication

This cookbook is dedicated to the memory and spirit of Sam Haines (WindSong Bed & Breakfast), whose love for innkeeping and cooking inspired his peers and delighted his guests.

Acknowledgements

This book is the second cookbook we have published featuring recipes from the members of the Washington Bed & Breakfast Guild. The first book, *A Taste Of Washington State*, included many wonderful recipes and was very popular. This new book contains even more recipes, and we trust that it is a book you will use often. We would like to thank the following people for making this book a reality:

- The participating innkeepers who took the time to share some of their favorite and most popular recipes.

- Leslie Lohse, Stratford Manor
  Gerry Flaten, Soundview Bed & Breakfast
  Cookbook Co-Chairpersons

CONTENTS

Hints For Preparing Your Breakfast Meal

1. Try serving foods with opposite flavors (i.e. bland vs. strong flavors). Very strong or different tastes will cancel one another out.

2. Try varying the textures of foods served (i.e. present a variety of those that are soft, crisp or creamy). Further, vary the colors of food that you serve.

3. Serve both cold and hot foods. This means even in summer, serve something hot and even in winter, serve something cold.

4. Spicy or tart foods served first will stimulate the appetite. Sweet foods served last will help to deaden the appetite.

5. Season your food selectively. Work to bring out the natural flavors. (You can enhance flavors by using fresh herbs from your backyard garden or getting fresh herbs from a local Farmers Market.) The basic spices can be added individually if you put a salt and pepper shaker on the table.

6. The sight of food alone is stimulating to the appetite. However, you can make it more appealing by serving foods of contrasting color and shapes.

7. Have fun with the finishing touch -- your garnish for the plate. Again, use fresh herbs or mints from your garden. Also, you can slice thin pieces of fruit as a garnish and then add the final touch . . . a fresh, edible flower from your garden.

Fruit - Soup - Beverages

Melissa Pigg ©

The Art of Napkin Folding

The art of napkin folding goes back in history, when someone discovered that napkins could be more than just functional accessories at a table. Creatively folded and presented they entice the diner to try the meal and add a touch of elegance to the occasion. Besides providing a topic of conversation, they show that the hostess possesses both thoughtfulness and imagination. Some of the folds presented may already be familiar to you, but it is always fun to do them anyway.

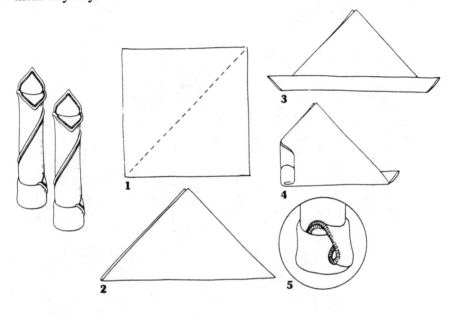

Candle

1. Form a triangle by folding in half.

2. Place the napkin as illustrated.

3. Fold up the bottom edge about one and one-half inches.

4. Turn the napkin over and roll it as shown.

5. Stand the napkin upright and tuck the corner into the cuff to hold the shape in place. Fold down one layer at the tip of the candle to complete.

♥ # Cranapple Smoothie ♥

1 cup cranapple juice
1 cup vanilla yogurt

1 banana
1/4 cup crushed ice

Blend ingredients together until thoroughly blended and smooth.

Submitted by All Seasons River Inn, Leavenworth

♥ # Five Berry Frappé ♥

1 banana
2 cups frozen berries
(strawberries, boysen-
berries, blueberries,
blackberries, and
raspberries)

3/4 cup plain, vanilla,
or berry yogurt
1 cup or more juice
(cranberry, cran-
raspberry, orange, etc.)

Put banana, berries, yogurt, and a splash of juice in 1 quart blender and process at high speed until smooth. Continue adding juice until the right consistency is reached. We like it to be like a thick, smooth milkshake.

Submitted by Ravenscroft Inn, Port Townsend

♥ # Fruit & Yogurt Smoothies ♥

1 - 2 bananas
1 cup fresh or frozen
strawberries
1 kiwi, peeled
4 - 6 fresh or frozen
apricots

1 cup crushed pineapple
1/2 cup orange juice
1/2 - 3/4 cup vanilla
yogurt
1 teaspoon vanilla
Lime slices for garnish

Chill all ingredients except vanilla. Place all ingredients into blender and crush until well blended. Serve in chilled glasses with a slice of lime. Makes approximately 4 cups.

Submitted by Bosch Gärten B&B, Leavenworth

♥   Mike's Fruit Drink   ♥

1 (6-ounce) can frozen quality concentrated orange juice (fill container 3 times with ice instead of water)

1 banana (banana can be frozen or fresh)
4 strawberries
4 raspberries
Orange zest

Put orange juice concentrate, ice, banana, strawberries, and raspberries in blender on low speed until ice is crushed. Add 4 slices of julienned orange zest into blender - high speed to fluff. Makes 6 - 8 servings.

Submitted by Nantucket Inn, Anacortes

♥   Blackberry Soup   ♥

2 cups fresh or frozen blackberries
1/3 cup sugar
1 tablespoon lemon juice
1 cinnamon stick

2 1/4 cups water, divided
2 tablespoons potato starch or cornstarch
Yogurt, berry leaves, and lemon peel for garnish

Bring berries, sugar, lemon juice, cinnamon stick, and 2 cups water to a boil. Reduce heat, cover and simmer for 10 minutes. Strain mixture through cheesecloth, discard pulp, and cinnamon stick. Taste strained juice. Add additional sugar and lemon juice to bring to 2 cups juice. In saucepan stir together starch (if cornstarch is used, soup will be opaque) and 1/4 cup water. Cook and stir until thickened and bubbly (2 to 3 minutes). Add juice mixture. Cook and stir until thickened. Do not boil. Cover surface with plastic wrap. Cool and refrigerate. Use yogurt to create a squiggle or heart; sprinkle with lemon zest, or create a flower with yogurt and use berry leaf and thin lemon slice for eye appeal.

Submitted by Ravenscroft Inn, Port Townsend

♥ Blender Blueberry Soup ♥

1 cup nonfat sour cream
3 (10-ounce) pkgs. frozen
   blueberries, partially
   thawed
6 tablespoons sugar

Dash of ginger,
   cinnamon, or dried
   mint (opt.)
Lemon slices, for
   garnish

In covered blender container at low speed, whirl sour cream, blueberries, and sugar until creamy smooth. May add dash of ginger, cinnamon, or dried mint, if desired. Serve in chilled bowls, garnished with lemon slices. Can make ahead and keep chilled several hours. Makes 6 servings.

Submitted by Reflections B&B, Port Orchard

♥ Butternut Squash Soup ♥

1 butternut squash,
   peeled, seeded, and
   diced
1 quart chicken broth
1/8 teaspoon ground
   cloves
1/8 teaspoon ground
   nutmeg
1/8 teaspoon ground
   cinnamon

1/4 teaspoon thyme
1/4 teaspoon curry
   powder
1/4 cup brown sugar
1/2 cup cranberries
1/2 cup hazelnuts
2 cups heavy cream
2 tablespoons chopped
   parsley
Salt & pepper, to taste

Peel, seed, and dice butternut squash. Place squash, broth, spices, herbs, and brown sugar, into heavy kettle. Bring to a boil and reduce to a simmer. Simmer covered until squash is very tender (about 45 minutes). Add chopped cranberries and hazelnuts to the simmering squash and cook for 8 to 10 minutes. Stir in cream and parsley. Season with salt and pepper, to taste.

Submitted by The Orcas Hotel, Orcas Island

♥ # Cold Raspberry Soup ♥

4 (10-ounce) pkgs. frozen raspberries, thawed
2 cups port wine

4 short cinnamon sticks
2 teaspoons cornstarch
1/2 cup water

In 3 quart saucepan over medium heat, heat raspberries, port, and cinnamon sticks just to boiling. Reduce heat to low and simmer for 10 minutes. Mix cornstarch and water together. Stir slowly into soup. Cook until thickened, stirring. Cover and refrigerate. To serve, remove cinnamon sticks, and ladle into chilled bowls. Add a dollop of plain yogurt. Garnish with fresh mint. Makes 6 servings.

Submitted by Reflections B&B, Port Orchard

♥ # Danish Apple Soup ♥

3 cups apples, diced
2 cups chicken broth
2 cinnamon sticks
Salt, to taste (opt.)
1/2 cup brown sugar

1/2 cup granulated sugar
1 tablespoon cornstarch
1/2 cup red wine
Whipped cream
Ground cinnamon

Simmer covered diced apples, chicken broth, cinnamon sticks, and salt, if desired, until apples are soft. Remove cinnamon sticks and mash or whirl apple mixture in blender. Add brown sugar, sugar, and cornstarch mixed with red wine. Taste for sweetness, adding more sugar if needed. Heat or chill. Top each serving with a dollop of whipped cream. Sprinkle with ground cinnamon. Makes 6 servings.

Submitted by Reflections B&B, Port Orchard

♥   Creamed Rice (With Fruit Soup)   ♥

1 cup rice	1/2 teaspoon salt
1 cup water	7 additional cups milk
1 cup milk	1/2 cup sugar

Combine first four ingredients in large microwave-safe bowl. Heat in microwave on High about 7 minutes. Stir. Heat 7 more minutes and stir. Add 1 cup milk; heat 7 more minutes. Stir. Repeat until all of the additional milk is added. Remove from microwave and add sugar. Serve topped with Danish Rhubarb-Strawberry Soup. (See recipe at bottom of page.) If desired, freeze in portion-sized servings. Makes 10 servings.

Submitted by Scandinavian Gardens Inn, Long Beach Peninsula

♥   Danish Rhubarb-Strawberry Soup   ♥
(With Creamed Rice)

12 stalks rhubarb (about 2 pounds), cut into 1" pieces	2 tablespoons lemon juice
Water to cover rhubarb	4 cups sugar, or to taste
2 pounds whole frozen strawberries	1 can whole cranberry sauce
1 cinnamon stick	2 tablespoons cornstarch

Place cut rhubarb into large saucepan with enough water to cover. Cook until tender. Add strawberries, cinnamon, lemon juice, and cranberry sauce. Bring to a boil. Add sugar to taste. Add cornstarch mixed with a little water and cook about 5 minutes. Serve over Creamed Rice. (See recipe at top of page.) Freezes great.

Submitted by Scandinavian Gardens Inn, Long Beach Peninsula

♥ Wild Rice Mushroom Soup ♥

1 cup fresh sliced
mushrooms
1/2 cup sliced green
onion
1 teaspoon minced garlic
3 cups chicken stock or
broth (stock preferred)
1/3 cup wild rice
1 cup half and half or
light cream

2 tablespoons flour
1 teaspoon snipped fresh
thyme or 1/2 teaspoon
dried thyme
1/8 teaspoon
pepper
1/2 teaspoon salt
1 tablespoon sherry

Sauté mushrooms, onion and garlic together. In large pan combine chicken stock and uncooked wild rice. Bring to a boil, reduce heat and simmer, covered, for 40 minutes. Combine half and half or light cream, flour, thyme, pepper and salt. Stir into the rice/stock base, then add the mushroom, onion and garlic sauté. Cook and stir until thick and bubbly. Stir in sherry and heat throughout. Makes 4 servings. Note: Don't be tempted to add more rice, it gets too gummy and sticky.

Submitted by Edenwild Inn, Lopez Island

♥ Apple Crisp ♥

6 - 8 Granny Smith or
other green apples,
sliced
1 cup flour
1 cup oats

1 cup brown sugar
1/4 cup white sugar
1 teaspoon cinnamon
1 teaspoon nutmeg
1/2 cup butter, melted

Slice apples into buttered baking dish. Mix dry ingredients, and add melted butter. Sprinkle over apples. Bake at 350° for 30 to 45 minutes.

Submitted by Argyle House B&B, San Juan Island

♥ Apples With Granola & Cider Cream ♥

Cinnamon-sugar mixture, to taste
4 large apples (reds, goldens, Braeburn or Fuji)
1/2 cup dried cranberries

4 cups Quaker 100% Natural Granola ® (or your favorite)
8 tablespoons melted butter, plus extra for buttering dish

Cider Cream:
1 cup apple cider

1 cup whipping cream

Generously butter 9" x 9" glass pan or 8 large ramekins. Sprinkle bottom of pans with cinnamon-sugar. Peel, halve, core and slice apples about 1/4" thick. Maintain shape of apple half and place in dish. Sprinkle tops of apples with more cinnamon-sugar and dried cranberries. Pour 1/4 cup granola on each apple half. Pour melted butter onto granola. Cover with foil and bake at 350° for 45 to 60 minutes. To make Cider Cream: Boil cider until reduced to 1/4 cup. Cool. Beat cream until stiff. Blend in cider syrup. Makes 8 servings. Serve apples topped with Cider Cream and dash of cinnamon.

Submitted by Autumn Pond B&B, Leavenworth

♥ Baked Apple ♥

1 cooking apple, per serving (Rome or other cooking apple)
1 tablespoon brown sugar stuffing mix (see below)

1 teaspoon apricot brandy
1/2 teaspoon butter
Dab of sweetened whipped cream
Sprig of mint

Brown Sugar Stuffing:
1/2 cup brown sugar
1 tablespoon cinnamon

2 tablespoons ground nuts

Core apples and peel the tops one-third down. Cut a slice off the bottom so the apples set level. For Brown Sugar Stuffing Mix: Stir ingredients together until well blended. (This recipe will fill approximately 12 apples.) Place apples in baking dish; fill cavities with brown sugar stuffing mix. Pour brandy over stuffing, top with butter. Add 1/2" to 1" water to baking pan and bake at 350° for 1 hour. Top with sweetened whipped cream and sprig of mint.

Submitted by Gaylord House, Everett

♥ ## Baked Apples Supreme ♥

8 cooking apples (Granny
 Smith are good)
1/2 cup dried cranberries
1/2 cup dried apricots,
 chopped
1/2 cup raisins

1/2 cup chopped
 pecans
1 teaspoon cinnamon
1/2 teaspoon nutmeg
1 cup apple juice
Caramel apple dip

Wash and core apples; peel a strip from top of each. Mix cranberries, apricots, raisins, pecans, cinnamon, and nutmeg. Fill centers of apples with fruit mixture. Place apples in casserole dish. Add apple juice to dish. Bake covered at 325° for about 1 hour or until tender. Top each apple with caramel dip while apples are piping hot. Serve apples warm with a dollop of whipped cream and mint sprig. Makes 8 servings.

Submitted by Green Gables Inn, Walla Walla

♥ ## Baked Bosc Pears ♥

1 large Bosc pear, per
 serving
Brown sugar, to taste

Vanilla, to taste
Pecans for garnish,
 to taste

Cut pear in half and core lengthwise. Place in pie plate and microwave on high for 3 to 4 minutes, depending on how ripe they are. Remove from microwave and add brown sugar and vanilla, to taste. Garnish with pecans. Place back in microwave on high for 30 seconds. Serve warm. Guests love them for breakfast.

Submitted by The Farm, a B&B, Trout Lake

Baked Peaches With Raspberry Puree

1/2 (10-ounce) pkg.
  frozen raspberries in
  light syrup, slightly
  thawed
1 1/2 teaspoons lemon
  juice
2 medium peaches,
  peeled, halved & pitted
  or 4 canned peach
  halves

1 1/2 tablespoons
  brown sugar
1/4 teaspoon ground
  cinnamon
1/2 teaspoon rum or
  rum flavoring
1 1/2 teaspoons
  butter

Combine raspberries and lemon juice in container of electric blender or food processor; cover and process until smooth. Strain raspberry puree; discard seeds. Cover and chill. Place peach halves in baking dish, cut side up. Combine brown sugar and cinnamon; spoon over peaches. Sprinkle with rum or rum flavoring, dot with butter. Cover with foil and bake at 350° for 10 to 15 minutes or until thoroughly heated. To serve, spoon 2 tablespoons raspberry puree over each grilled peach half. Makes 4 servings.

Submitted by Apple Country B&B, Wenatchee

Bluebarb Crunch

4 cups rhubarb, cut into
  1" pieces
2 cups blueberries
1 cup sugar
1/2 cup flour
1 teaspoon cinnamon
1 teaspoon lemon juice
1/2 cup water

Topping:
1 cup flour
1 cup brown sugar
1/2 cup melted
  butter
1/2 cup quick oats
1/2 cup chopped walnuts
  (opt.)

Preheat oven to 375°. Mix together fruit, sugar, flour, cinnamon, lemon juice, and water. Put into greased 9" x 12" baking dish. Sprinkle with topping. Bake for 45 minutes or until rhubarb is tender. Serve warm with cream. Makes 8 servings.

Submitted by Schnauzer Crossing, Bellingham

♥　　　　**Blueberry Breakfast Pudding**　　　　♥

1 large egg
1/3 cup light brown sugar
1 cup skim milk
1 teaspoon ground
　cinnamon
1 teaspoon grated lemon
　rind
Pinch of ground nutmeg

1 teaspoon vanilla
6 slices whole wheat
　bread, torn into 1/2"
　pieces
2 cups fresh or frozen
　blueberries
1/2 cup plain lowfat
　yogurt (opt.)

With fork beat egg and brown sugar together in large bowl until well blended. Stir in milk, cinnamon, lemon rind, nutmeg and vanilla. Tear bread into 1/2" pieces, add to mixture and stir. Cover and refrigerate for 1 hour or overnight. Preheat oven to 375°. Lightly coat an 8" x 8" x 2" baking pan with cooking spray. Stir the blueberries into the bread mixture and spoon into pan. Bake for 40 minutes or until firm. Serve warm, topping each portion with 2 tablespoons of yogurt, if desired. Makes 6 servings.

Submitted by Glenna's Guthrie Cottage B&B, Sequim

♥　　　**Boreas Stuffed Butter Rum Pears**　　　♥

6 pears, cored
1/4 cup brown sugar
1/2 teaspoon cinnamon
1/8 teaspoon freshly
　grated nutmeg

1/2 cup dried cranberries
1/2 cup chopped pecans
Grand Marnier brandy or
　dark rum, to taste (opt.)
Butter, to taste

Core the pears and using a sharp knife, score a circle around the center of the pear, only piercing the skin (to allow steam to escape, preventing the pear from bursting). Mix together brown sugar, cinnamon, nutmeg, cranberries and pecans in small bowl. Stuff this mixture into the pears, packing lightly. If desired, you can pour Grand Marnier brandy or dark rum down the core of the pear. Top each pear with a blob of butter. Place pears in glass baking dish and add about 1/2" water to the dish. Bake pears at 350° for about 25 minutes depending upon the size of the pears. Baste occasionally while baking. You can make pears the night before, but don't add water until you bake them. Makes 6 luscious pears.

Submitted by Boreas B&B Inn, Long Beach

♥   # Cantaloupe With Ice Cream   ♥

1/2 cantaloupe, per two servings, scooped into melon balls
2 scoops vanilla ice cream, per two servings

Dash of nutmeg
Fresh mint and a strawberry, for garnish

Divide melon balls in 2 stemmed Margarita glasses. Put 1 scoop vanilla ice cream on top of each. Sprinkle dash of nutmeg over ice cream. Garnish with fresh mint and a strawberry (in season).

Submitted by The Fountains B&B, Gig Harbor

♥   # Fresh Fruit With Chocolate   ♥

Strawberries
Bananas
Apples
Pears
Kiwi

For Dipping:
Chocolate syrup
2 drops Grand Marnier

Fresh mint for garnish

Slice two or three fruits of your choice and arrange attractively on a saucer or salad plate. Pour chocolate syrup into bottom of stemware dessert glass, and drizzle a couple of drops of Grand Marnier over chocolate. Garnish with fresh mint.

Submitted by The Fountains B&B, Gig Harbor

♥ # Fruit Casserole ♥

1 medium can peach	2 tablespoons flour
halves	1/2 cup brown
1 medium can pear halves	sugar
1 medium can apricot	1 cup cooking sherry
halves	1 teaspoon curry
1 medium can pineapple	1/4 teaspoon cinnamon
chunks	1/4 teaspoon cloves
1/2 stick butter, melted	1 jar red apple rings

Drain fruit and reserve juice. Melt butter in saucepan. When almost sizzling, add flour and stir until completely blended with butter. Add 1 1/2 cups combined juices from the fruit. Cook and stir with wire whisk until thick. Add brown sugar, sherry, and spices. Arrange all fruit, except apple rings, in large casserole; pour sauce over all, and put apple rings on top. Bake at 300° for 25 minutes. May make a day ahead if desired.

Submitted by Samish Point by the Bay, La Conner (Mt. Vernon)

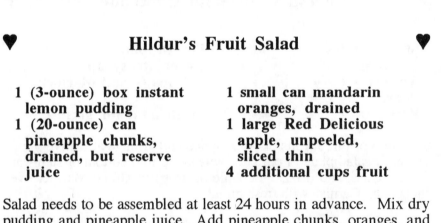

♥ # Hildur's Fruit Salad ♥

1 (3-ounce) box instant	1 small can mandarin
lemon pudding	oranges, drained
1 (20-ounce) can	1 large Red Delicious
pineapple chunks,	apple, unpeeled,
drained, but reserve	sliced thin
juice	4 additional cups fruit

Salad needs to be assembled at least 24 hours in advance. Mix dry pudding and pineapple juice. Add pineapple chunks, oranges, and thinly sliced apples. Add 4 additional cups of fruit of your choice on the day of serving.

Submitted by Mt. Higgins House, Darrington

♥   **Kiwi Peanut Butter Parfait**   ♥

1 kiwi fruit, per person

1 teaspoon peanut butter, per person

1 teaspoon vanilla yogurt, per person

1/4 teaspoon honey, per person

1/2 teaspoon applesauce, per person

1/2 teaspoon granola, per person

Peel kiwi fruit and slice 1/3 of fruit into the bottom of parfait glass. Mix peanut butter, vanilla yogurt, honey, and applesauce. Drop half of the mixture on the layer of kiwi, and sprinkle with granola. Repeat layers of kiwi, peanut butter mixture, and granola, finishing with a layer of kiwi. Top with vanilla yogurt and garnish with fruit or granola.

Submitted by All Seasons River Inn, Leavenworth

Hints For Fruit Garnishes:

Starfruit or carambolas are used for their golden yellow color and star shape when sliced. Four to six ribs run lengthwise on the surface of the starfruit. It is crisp and has a sweet-tart flavor. Wash this fruit and slice it to use as an attractive plate garnish.

Kiwi or Chinese gooseberry comes from New Zealand, but is also grown in California today. Peel kiwi and slice it to use as a garnish. You can also cut it up to add color and flavor to a fruit salad.

♥ ## Marinated Fruit Salad ♥

3 large apples
1 small pineapple
1 small cantaloupe
1 medium bunch green or
  red grapes, seedless
1 pint strawberries,
  washed & hulled
Mint leaves

1/2 cup sugar
1 cup water
1/2 teaspoon lemon juice
2 cinnamon sticks
1/2 teaspoon whole
  cloves
1/2 teaspoon whole
  allspice

Cut fruit into bite-sized pieces (should be 2 cups each variety). Do not add strawberries and mint yet. Place fruit into large bowl. For Spice Marinade: In small saucepan combine sugar, water, lemon juice, and cinnamon sticks. Tie cloves and allspice in cheesecloth and add to saucepan. Bring to a boil, then lower to simmer for 5 minutes. Remove from heat and cool. Remove cinnamon sticks and spice bag. Pour marinade over fruit, cover and refrigerate overnight. Before serving, stir in strawberries and mint. Makes 12 servings.

Submitted by Childs' House B&B, Olalla

♥ ## Poached Pears ♥

4 fresh Bartlett pears,
  peeled & cored
2 cups water

2 tablespoons lemon juice
1 cinnamon stick
2 whole cloves

In large microwave-safe casserole, place pears, water, lemon juice, cinnamon, and cloves. Cover with plastic wrap, venting one corner. Microwave on high for 5 to 7 minutes. Drain pears. To serve, place pears on individual serving plates and spoon raspberry purée over them. Garnish with a sprig of mint. Makes 4 servings. Note: Use a potato peeler to easily peel pears. Slice a little off the bottom of each pear so they will stand up nicely on the plate.

Submitted by Commencement Bay B&B, Tacoma

♥ Sautéed Bananas With Brandy Cream Sauce ♥

4 tablespoons butter
1/2 cup packed brown
 sugar

4 ripe bananas, cut in half
 lengthwise and across
Cinnamon, to taste

Brandy Cream Sauce:
1 cup heavy cream
3 tablespoons
 confectioners sugar

1 tablespoon
 brandy

In medium skillet melt butter with brown sugar. Add sliced bananas and sauté for 5 minutes until tender, turning once. For Brandy Cream Sauce: Mix ingredients together until thickened. Makes 1 cup sauce. Place bananas in serving dishes and pour Brandy Cream Sauce over the top. Sprinkle with cinnamon and serve immediately.

Submitted by BJ's Garden Gate, Port Angeles

Hints On Fresh Fruit:

Some fruits are known for ripening after being picked. These include apricots, bananas, melons, mangoes, nectarines, peaches, pears, strawberries to a limited extent, and pineapples. None of these, however, will become sweeter in flavor. Store these fruits at room temperature in a dark place. Ripening will be faster if each type of fruit is kept in a partly closed paper bag. When ripened, you should chill the fruit in your refrigerator before serving.

Almost all fresh fruits lose their flavor rapidly when soaked in water. Always wash fruit quickly under slow flowing water just before using and dry off thoroughly.

Equivalents:

4 medium apples = 4 cups sliced apples
1 pint strawberries = 2 cups strawberries
4 cups unpitted cherries = 2 cups pitted cherries
8 medium peaches = 4 cups sliced peaches

♥ Shepherd's Inn Pasta/Fruit Breakfast Salad ♥

1 1/2 cups sugar
3 tablespoons flour
2 1/2 teaspoons salt
2 1/2 cups pineapple juice
3 eggs, beaten
2 tablespoons lemon juice
3 quarts water
1 tablespoon oil
1 (16-ounce) pkg.
  Ronzoni Acini Pepe®
  pasta
2 (20-ounce) cans
  pineapple chunks,
  drained

1 (20-ounce) can crushed
  pineapple, drained
3 (11-ounce) cans
  mandarin oranges,
  drained
1 (9-ounce) carton
  non-dairy whipped
  topping
1/2 cup coconut (opt.)
Red seedless grapes,
  or any desired fresh
  fruit, as garnish
  before serving

Combine sugar, flour, and 1/2 teaspoon salt. Gradually stir in pineapple juice and eggs. Cook over medium heat until thickened. Add lemon juice. Cool mixture to room temperature. Bring water, 2 teaspoons salt, and oil, to a boil. Add soup pasta. Cook at rolling boil until done. Drain, rinse with water, drain again, and cool to room temperature. Combine pasta and cooled egg mixture. Mix lightly but thoroughly. Refrigerate overnight in airtight container. Add remaining ingredients except fresh fruit. Refrigerate until chilled. Salad may be kept refrigerated for a week in airtight container. When ready to serve, remove the amount you need. Add red grapes for color, fresh banana chunks if desired, or you may experiment with other fruit. This makes nearly a gallon. Can be made ahead, tastes great, looks beautiful, and is a snap to serve on busy days. (Acini Pepe® can be found in Safeway Stores.)

Submitted by The Shepherd's Inn B&B, Salkum

♥ ## Snappy Peaches ♥

1 fresh peach, per serving
1/2 - 1 teaspoon pepper-
mint Schnapp's liqueur,
per serving

Sugar, to taste
Fresh mint leaf, fresh
raspberries, or edible
flowers for garnish

Slice peaches, add peppermint Schnapp's, and sugar. Chill well. Serve alone or over cream custard. Garnish with fresh mint leaf, fresh raspberries, and/or edible flowers.

Submitted by Foxbridge B&B, Poulsbo

♥ ## Spiced Fruit ♥

1/2 medium jicama or
star fruit, peeled & cut
into 1/4" slices
3 medium oranges,
peeled & sliced 1/4"
thick

3 medium kiwi fruit,
peeled & sliced
1/4 cup dried
cranberries

Orange Honey Dressing:
1/4 cup orange juice
1/4 cup honey

1/2 teaspoon ground
cinnamon

Prepare Orange Honey Dressing by mixing together all ingredients. Cut jicama into star shape using cookie cutter (or use star fruit). Mix all fruit (except cranberries) together in bowl. Top with dressing. Chill overnight if desired. Top with dried cranberries. Use as an accompaniment with dishes you are serving.

Submitted by The Churchyard Inn, Uniontown

♥ Warm Winter Fruit Compote ♥

2 ripe pears or apples,
  peeled & cored
1 1/2 teaspoons lemon
  juice
1/4 cup apple juice

2 tablespoons sugar
1/2 cup cranberries,
  fresh or frozen
2 tablespoons golden
  raisins

Peel and core fruit. Slice each into 8 equal wedges or into large, even chunks. Sprinkle fruit pieces with lemon juice. In non-reactive saucepan over medium heat, dissolve sugar in apple juice. Add cranberries, cover, and simmer 2 to 3 minutes until cranberries soften and begin to color the juice. Add raisins and pears or apples. Reduce heat, cover and simmer for 5 minutes. Remove cover, stir gently with rubber spatula and continue simmering for up to 5 more minutes. Timing depends on ripeness of fruit. Cook until tender, not mushy. Makes 2 - 3 servings.

Submitted by The Bradley House, Cathlamet

♥ Fresh Raspberry Curd ♥

1 cup raspberries
2 tablespoons lemon juice
1/2 cup butter or
  margarine

3 tablespoons sugar
4 large eggs
Several drops red food
  coloring (opt.)

In food processor or blender, whirl raspberries with lemon juice until puréed. Pour into a fine strainer set over a measuring cup. Stir with a spoon to force pulp through strainer; discard seeds. You need 1/2 cup purée. Melt butter in 2 - 3 quart pan over medium heat. Add raspberry purée, sugar, and eggs. Reduce heat to low and stir constantly until sauce is thickened and smooth, about 10 minutes for a deeper color. Stir in food coloring a few drops at a time. Let cool, then cover and refrigerate until thickened, about 1 hour.

Submitted by Marianna Stoltz House B&B, Spokane

♥ ## Mandarin Strawberry Topping ♥

1 (11-ounce) can
  mandarin oranges,
  drained
1 (10-ounce) pkg. frozen
  strawberry halves,
  thawed & drained

Water, as needed
2 tablespoons sugar
1 tablespoon plus 1 1/2
  teaspoons cornstarch
1 teaspoon lemon juice

Drain orange segments and strawberries, reserving syrups. Add water to reserved syrups to measure 1 1/2 cups liquid. Combine sugar, cornstarch, and syrup mixture in medium saucepan. Bring to a boil over medium-high heat. Stirring constantly, boil and stir for 1 minute. Stir in lemon juice, orange segments, and strawberries. Serve with pancakes, waffles, or French toast.

Submitted by Marianna Stoltz House B&B, Spokane

♥ ## Nonfat Orange Yogurt Topping ♥

1 (8-ounce) carton vanilla
  or plain nonfat yogurt
1 tablespoon grated
  orange zest

1 teaspoon grated lemon
  zest
1/4 cup orange juice
  concentrate, thawed

Mix all ingredients together until smooth. Do not dilute orange juice. Chill for several hours or overnight to allow flavor to intensify. Serve over fresh berries, melon wedges, or mixed fruit compotes.

Submitted by The Bradley House, Cathlamet

♥ ## Paula's Pineapple Sorbet ♥

1/2 cup water
1/2 cup sugar
1/2 fresh pineapple
1 large banana, sliced

1/4 cup lemon juice
2 tablespoons orange
   liqueur or orange juice
Favorite mint sprigs

Bring water and sugar to a boil, stirring to dissolve sugar. Simmer without stirring for 3 minutes; cool to room temperature. Peel and core pineapple. Cut into chunks and blend in blender until smooth. Add banana, lemon juice, liqueur or orange juice, and process until smooth. Freeze in shallow container until frozen about 1 1/2 inches around edge. Process again in blender until smooth. Pour into freezer container and store in freezer until ready to serve. I use small melon ball size scoops in bowl with fruit sliced over top. Garnish with mint. You can substitute favorite fruits in season.

Submitted by Island Escape B&B, Gig Harbor Area

♥ ## Raspberry Puree ♥

1 cup fresh or frozen
   raspberries

1 tablespoon sugar,
   or to taste

Place raspberries and sugar in small microwave-safe bowl. Cover and microwave on high about 2 minutes or until mixture boils. Strain to remove seeds. Cool. Use to top Peach Melba Dutch Babies, waffles, French toast, pancakes, ice cream, or poached pears.

Submitted by Commencement Bay B&B, Tacoma

♥ ## Vanilla Fruit Topping ♥

1 cup sugar
1/2 cup heavy cream

1/2 cup butter
1 teaspoon vanilla

Combine sugar, heavy cream, butter, and vanilla in medium saucepan. Bring to boil over medium-high heat. Cook, stirring, for approximately 3 minutes. Pour into heat-resistant container and let cool. Serve over favorite fresh fruits.

Submitted by Channel House, Anacortes

Muffins ~ Scones ~ Biscuits

Melissa Pigg ©

Napkin Folding

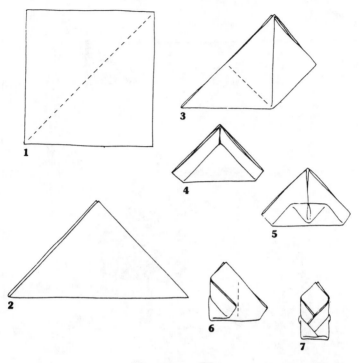

Butterfly

1. Fold the napkin in half diagonally to form a triangle.
2. Place the fold along the bottom edge.
3. Hold your finger at the center of the bottom edge as you fold the right and left corners up to the top corner.
4. Fold up the bottom point to within one inch of the top point.
5. Fold the same point back to the bottom edge.
6. Turn the napkin over and fold the left side toward the center.
7. Fold the right side over the left side, tucking the point into the left fold. Stand the napkin up.
8. Pull down the left and right sides of the napkin until they are horizontal.

♥ ## Buttermilk Biscuits ♥

4 cups flour
2 teaspoons salt
4 teaspoons baking
  powder

4 tablespoons sugar
1 teaspoon baking soda
10 tablespoons butter
1 2/3 cups buttermilk

Sift first five ingredients together into very large bowl. Cut in butter. Lightly mix in buttermilk. Pat dough 1/2" thick. Cut out biscuits with heart-shaped cookie cutter. Knead dough together and cut out biscuits until all dough is used. Bake in top third of oven at 450° for 10 to 12 minutes. Makes 20 - 2" heart biscuits.

Submitted by Olympic Lights, San Juan Island

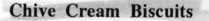

♥ ## Chive Cream Biscuits ♥

2 cups flour
2 teaspoons
  sugar
1/2 teaspoon salt
1 tablespoon baking
  powder

1/4 cup scallion greens,
  finely minced
1 1/2 cups whipping
  cream
5 tablespoons butter,
  melted

Preheat oven to 425°. Combine dry ingredients and scallions and mix. Pour in cream and mix. Knead by folding dough over on itself about 8 to 10 times. Roll dough to 1/2" thickness and cut out biscuits. Dip biscuits in melted butter and cook on parchment paper on baking pan for 13 to 15 minutes. Makes about 20 tiny (1 3/4") biscuits. Serve hot.

Submitted by WindSong Inn, Orcas Island, San Juan Islands

♥ ## Corn Biscuits ♥

4 cups flour
1 cup yellow cornmeal
2 teaspoons baking soda
2 teaspoons salt
4 tablespoons sugar

5 teaspoons baking powder
16 tablespoons (8 ounces) butter
2 cups + 3 tablespoons buttermilk

Sift together first six ingredients. Cut in butter. Add buttermilk all at once. Mix very lightly. Turn out onto floured board. Pat dough out to 1/2" thick. Cut out biscuits; place on flat cookie sheet not too close together. Bake in the top third of oven at 450° for about 10 minutes. Makes 34 small biscuits about 2" in diameter.

Submitted by Olympic Lights, San Juan Island

♥ ## Low-Fat Popovers ♥

1 cup all purpose flour
2 tablespoons sugar
1/4 teaspoon salt
1 tablespoon canola oil
1 teaspoon grated orange peel

1/2 teaspoon orange flavoring
1/4 teaspoon almond flavoring
4 egg whites
1 cup non-fat milk

Spray muffin tins with cooking oil spray. In small bowl, combine flour, sugar, and salt; set aside. In electric mixing bowl, combine canola oil, orange peel, flavorings, egg whites, and milk. Beat until well-blended. Add flour mixture, blending well. Pour into sprayed muffin tins. Bake at 350° for 35 minutes. Makes 12 popovers.

Submitted by Tower House B&B, San Juan Island

♥ ## Banana-Date Bran Muffins ♥

1 cup All-Bran® cereal
1 1/4 cups flour
1/4 cup sugar
1 teaspoon baking soda
1/4 teaspoon salt
1/2 cup chopped, pitted
   dates

1/4 cup milk
3 bananas, mashed
2 eggs, beaten
4 tablespoons melted
   butter
1 teaspoon vanilla

Preheat oven to 400°. Grease muffin tin. Mix together cereal, flour, sugar, baking soda, salt, and dates. In separate bowl mix together milk, bananas, eggs, melted butter, and vanilla. Pour into flour mixture and stir until just combined (do not overmix). Pour into muffin pan and bake for 20 minutes until golden. Cool on wire rack. (These also freeze well, but completely cool first!)

Submitted by Tudor Inn, Port Angeles

♥ ## Blueberry Bran Muffins ♥

4 cups unprocessed bran
4 cups flour
2 cups sugar
2 teaspoons salt
4 teaspoons baking
   powder

3 eggs
1 1/2 cups canola oil
4 cups non-fat milk
Raisins, to taste
Blueberries, to
   taste

Preheat oven to 425°. Mix together dry ingredients; separately mix together wet ingredients. Combine two mixtures. When ready to bake, pour a quarter of the batter (for 12 muffins) into bowl and add generous amount of raisins and blueberries. Fill greased muffin pans almost full. Bake for 17 to 20 minutes. Batter can be refrigerated up to 2 weeks. Makes 3 1/2 - 4 dozen muffins.

Submitted by Schnauzer Crossing, Bellingham

♥ ## Blueberry Muffin Cakes ♥

1/2 cup softened
  Imperial® margarine
3/4 cup granulated sugar
2 eggs
2 1/3 cups flour
2 1/2 teaspoons baking
  powder
1/2 teaspoon salt

1/2 teaspoon ground
  nutmeg
3/4 cup milk
1 1/2 cups blueberries
Topping:
1/2 cup melted butter
1/4 teaspoon cinnamon
3/4 cup sugar

In mixing bowl cream margarine and sugar, and then beat in eggs. Mix together flour, baking powder, salt, and nutmeg. Add to margarine, alternating with milk. Fold in blueberries and spoon into greased muffin tins. Bake at 350° for 20 to 25 minutes. Cool slightly after removing from muffin tins. Roll first in melted butter and then in cinnamon-sugar mixture. Makes 18 cakes.

Submitted by Katy's Inn, La Conner

♥ ## Blueberry Pumpkin Muffins ♥

1 2/3 cups flour
1 teaspoon baking soda
1/2 teaspoon baking
  powder
1/2 teaspoon salt
1 teaspoon cinnamon
1/2 teaspoon allspice
1 cup Libby's® pumpkin

1/4 cup evaporated
  milk
1/3 cup shortening
1 cup firmly packed light
  brown sugar
1 egg
1 cup blueberries
1 tablespoon flour

Streusel:
2 tablespoons flour
2 tablespoons sugar

1/4 teaspoon cinnamon
1 tablespoon butter

Combine first six ingredients. Combine pumpkin and evaporated milk until blended. Cream shortening and brown sugar in large mixing bowl. Add egg, beat until mixture is fluffy. Add flour mixture alternately with pumpkin mixture, beating well after each addition. Combine blueberries and 1 tablespoon flour. Gently stir into batter. Fill 18 greased muffin tins 3/4 full or make 6 muffins in extra large tins. For Streusel: Combine flour, sugar and cinnamon. Cut in butter until mixture is crumbly. Sprinkle streusel over top of muffins. Bake in electric oven at 350° for 40 minutes or in convection oven at 325° for 30 minutes until toothpick inserted in center comes out clean.

Submitted by The Green Cape Cod B&B, Tacoma

♥ Bran Muffins ♥

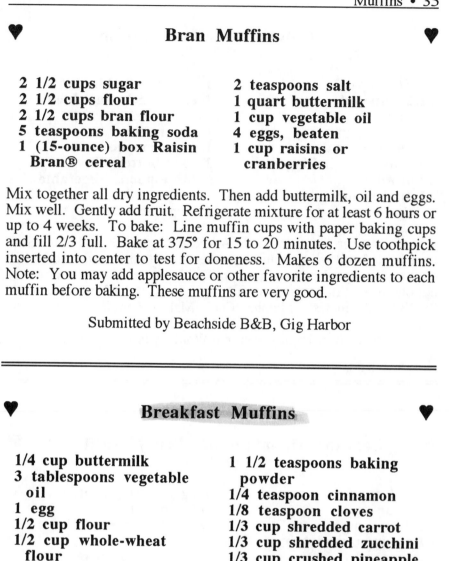

2 1/2 cups sugar
2 1/2 cups flour
2 1/2 cups bran flour
5 teaspoons baking soda
1 (15-ounce) box Raisin
Bran® cereal

2 teaspoons salt
1 quart buttermilk
1 cup vegetable oil
4 eggs, beaten
1 cup raisins or
cranberries

Mix together all dry ingredients. Then add buttermilk, oil and eggs. Mix well. Gently add fruit. Refrigerate mixture for at least 6 hours or up to 4 weeks. To bake: Line muffin cups with paper baking cups and fill 2/3 full. Bake at 375° for 15 to 20 minutes. Use toothpick inserted into center to test for doneness. Makes 6 dozen muffins. Note: You may add applesauce or other favorite ingredients to each muffin before baking. These muffins are very good.

Submitted by Beachside B&B, Gig Harbor

♥ Breakfast Muffins ♥

1/4 cup buttermilk
3 tablespoons vegetable
oil
1 egg
1/2 cup flour
1/2 cup whole-wheat
flour
1/3 cup sugar

1 1/2 teaspoons baking
powder
1/4 teaspoon cinnamon
1/8 teaspoon cloves
1/3 cup shredded carrot
1/3 cup shredded zucchini
1/3 cup crushed pineapple
1/4 cup sunflower seeds

In large bowl, beat buttermilk, vegetable oil, and egg. Stir in flour, whole-wheat flour, sugar, baking powder, cinnamon, and cloves. Fold in carrot, zucchini, pineapple, and sunflower seeds. Spoon batter into 6 greased muffin tins. Bake at 400° for 20 minutes.

Submitted by The Guest House B&B, Seattle

♥ Carrot-Raisin-Walnut Muffins ♥

3 1/2 cups flour
1/2 cup quick-cooking oats
3/4 cup sugar
1 teaspoon salt
2 teaspoons baking powder
1 tablespoon ground cinnamon
1 teaspoon baking soda
2 cups finely shredded carrot
1 cup raisins
1 cup chopped nuts
2 cups buttermilk
6 tablespoons vegetable oil
2 large eggs

Mix all dry ingredients in bowl. Add carrots, raisins, and nuts. Stir. In separate bowl whisk liquid ingredients until combined. Add all at once to dry ingredients and mix until all ingredients are just wet. Do not overmix. Fill greased muffin cups. Bake at 400° on center rack for 18 to 20 minutes until done. Cool. Makes 16 muffins.

Submitted by Eagles Nest Inn, Whidbey Island - Langley

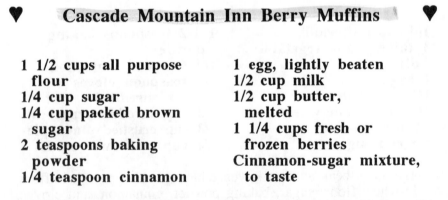

♥ Cascade Mountain Inn Berry Muffins ♥

1 1/2 cups all purpose flour
1/4 cup sugar
1/4 cup packed brown sugar
2 teaspoons baking powder
1/4 teaspoon cinnamon
1 egg, lightly beaten
1/2 cup milk
1/2 cup butter, melted
1 1/4 cups fresh or frozen berries
Cinnamon-sugar mixture, to taste

Combine first five ingredients. Add egg, milk and melted butter. Stir in berries. Fill greased muffin tins 2/3 full. Sprinkle lightly with cinnamon-sugar. Bake at 350° for 20 to 25 minutes until lightly brown and done to the touch. Makes 6 large or 12 small muffins.

Submitted by Cascade Mountain Inn, Concrete-Birdsview

♥ # Chunky Monkey Muffins ♥

1 cup walnuts, toasted & coarsely chopped

Cream Cheese Filling:
4 ounces soft cream cheese
2 tablespoons confectioners sugar
1 pinch of salt
1/2 cup semisweet chocolate chips

Muffin Batter:
2 cups all purpose flour
1 cup sugar
1/2 teaspoon salt
1 teaspoon baking powder
1 teaspoon baking soda
2 tablespoons salad oil
1 large egg
1/2 cup orange juice
2 large bananas, peeled
1 teaspoon vanilla

Preheat oven to 350°. Toast walnuts in preheating oven, then coarsely chop them and set aside. Prepare muffin papers for 16 muffins. Set pans aside. For Filling: Combine and cream well soft cream cheese, confectioners sugar and salt. Blend in chocolate chips. Set aside. For Muffin Batter: In bowl sift dry ingredients. Add chopped nuts. Set aside. In mixer bowl blend oil, egg, orange juice, bananas and vanilla. Slowly add dry ingredients and blend. Divide batter evenly between prepared muffin cups, reserving a small amount. Top each muffin with a teaspoon of the cream cheese filling and press down slightly. Put a small amount of reserved muffin batter on top of each muffin to cover cream cheese. Bake at 350° for 20 to 25 minutes.

Submitted by Kangaroo House B&B on Orcas Island,
Eastsound / Orcas Island

www.wbbg.com

♥ Chunky Pecan Muffins ♥

1 1/2 cups flour
2 teaspoons baking
  powder
1/4 teaspoon salt
Generous pinch of
  allspice
1 3/4 cups coarsely
  chopped toasted pecans

1/2 cup firmly packed
  dark brown sugar
1/2 cup (1 stick) butter,
  melted
1/3 cup milk
1/4 cup maple syrup
1 egg
1 teaspoon vanilla

Preheat oven to 400°. Generously grease 2 1/2" muffin cups or use baking cups. Mix flour, baking powder, salt, and allspice in large bowl. Stir in toasted pecans. Scoop out a well in center of dry ingredients. Whisk brown sugar, melted butter, milk, maple syrup, egg, and vanilla in medium bowl. Pour liquid ingredients into well, stir until just blended. Batter will be lumpy. Fill prepared muffin cups 3/4 full. Bake until muffins are golden brown and tester inserted in center comes out clean. Turn out, and serve warm.

Submitted by Ravenscroft Inn, Port Townsend

♥ Cinnamon Supremes ♥

2 cups all purpose flour
1 tablespoon baking
  powder
2 tablespoons cinnamon
1/4 teaspoon salt
2 large eggs

1 cup milk (skim is okay)
1/2 cup canola oil
1 cup packed brown
  sugar
1 cup chopped walnuts
1 cup raisins

Stir together flour, baking powder, cinnamon, and salt. Set aside. In another bowl beat eggs slightly, then mix in milk, canola oil, and brown sugar. Add this mixture to dry ingredients and mix quickly, stirring only until all flour is moistened. Gently stir in nuts and raisins. Spoon into 12 greased muffin cups. Bake at 375° for 18 minutes.

Submitted by The Bradley House, Cathlamet

♥ ## Cranberry Orange Muffins ♥

1/3 cup dried cranberries, chopped
2 tablespoons plus 1/3 cup sugar
3 tablespoons boiling water
1 3/4 cups flour
1/2 cup yellow cornmeal
2 1/2 teaspoons baking powder
1/2 teaspoon baking soda
1/2 teaspoon salt
2 eggs
1 cup milk
1/3 cup unsalted butter, melted
1 tablespoon grated orange peel

In small bowl stir together cranberries and 2 tablespoons sugar. Stir in boiling water; set aside for 15 minutes to soften cranberries. In large bowl mix flour, cornmeal, 1/3 cup sugar, baking powder, baking soda, and salt. In another bowl, whisk eggs lightly. Add milk, and melted butter, beat until smooth. Stir in cranberries, their liquid, and grated orange peel. Stir liquid mixture into flour mixture. Divide batter evenly among buttered muffin cups, filling each 3/4 full. Bake at 400° until risen and the tops golden, for 15 to 20 minutes. Let cool 2 to 3 minutes and serve warm. Makes 12 muffins.

Submitted by Water's Edge B&B, Gig Harbor

♥ ## Ginger-Peachy Muffins ♥

1/2 cup butter or margarine
1 1/4 cups sugar
1 teaspoon vanilla
2 eggs
2 cups flour
1/2 teaspoon salt
2 teaspoons baking powder
2 teaspoons ground ginger
1/2 cup milk
1 1/2 cups fresh, peeled, chopped, & drained peaches
1/2 cup pecans, chopped
Granulated sugar for topping

Preheat oven to 375°. Cream butter, sugar, and vanilla until light. Add eggs one at a time, beat well after each addition. Sift flour, salt, baking powder, and ginger together. Add to creamed mixture alternately with milk. Fold in peaches and pecans. Fill greased muffin tins 3/4 full with batter. Sprinkle tops lightly with granulated sugar. Bake for about 25 minutes. Cool before removing from muffin tins.

Submitted by White Swan Guest House, La Conner (Mt. Vernon)

♥ # Ham & Dijon Muffins ♥

1 2/3 cups all purpose
   flour
1/3 cup cornmeal
1/4 cup sugar
2 teaspoons baking
   powder
1/2 teaspoon salt
1/2 teaspoon baking
   soda
1/8 teaspoon ground
   cloves (opt.)
2 eggs
1 cup buttermilk
1/2 cup vegetable oil
1 - 2 teaspoons ground
   mustard
1 cup finely chopped,
   fully-cooked ham

In a bowl combine the first seven ingredients. Combine eggs, buttermilk, oil and mustard. Stir into dry ingredients until just moistened. Fold in ham and fill greased or paper-lined muffin cups 3/4 full. Bake at 375° for 20 to 25 minutes. Cool for 5 minutes on rack before removing from pans. Makes 12 - 14 muffins. Good with scrambled eggs or soups for lunch.

Submitted by The Log Castle B&B, Whidbey Island - Langley

♥ # Harvest Muffins ♥

2 cups flour
1/2 cup Quaker® oats
   (instant or regular)
1 tablespoon ground
   cinnamon
1 teaspoon baking soda
2 teaspoons baking
   powder
1 teaspoon powdered
   ginger
1 teaspoon salt
1 cup milk
1 grated carrot
1/2 cup brown sugar
1/2 cup raisins
1/2 cup fresh cranberries,
   chopped
1/2 cup vegetable oil
1 egg
2 tablespoons molasses

Preheat oven to 400°. Combine flour, oats, cinnamon, baking soda, baking powder, ginger, and salt in large bowl. In separate bowl stir together milk, carrot, brown sugar, raisins, cranberries, oil, egg, and molasses. Add wet ingredients to dry ingredients, stirring gently until just blended and lumpy. Pour batter into greased muffin tins, filling until just below rim. Bake until toothpick inserted in center comes out clean, for 15 to 20 minutes. Delicious served warm with cream cheese.

Submitted by White Swan Guest House, La Conner (Mt. Vernon)

♥ ## Jamie's Ginger Applesauce Muffins ♥

2 cups flour
3/4 cup brown sugar
1 tablespoon gingerroot
 or 1 teaspoon powdered
 ginger
1 teaspoon baking soda

1 teaspoon cinnamon
1 cup applesauce + 1/2
 cup molasses
1/2 cup oil
1 egg

Topping:
2 tablespoons flour
2 tablespoons brown
 sugar
1/2 teaspoon cinnamon

1 tablespoon melted
 butter
1 tablespoon chopped
 pecans

Preheat oven to 400°. Combine all dry ingredients in a large bowl. Combine all wet ingredients in a small bowl. Stir the two mixtures together until just mixed. Fill well-greased muffin tins 2/3 full with batter. Mix together topping ingredients and sprinkle on top of muffins. Bake for about 20 minutes. Makes 12 muffins.

Submitted by Edenwild Inn, Lopez Island

♥ ## Joanie Mann's Raw Apple Muffins ♥

4 cups diced apples
 (peeled or unpeeled)
1 cup sugar
2 eggs, beaten slightly
1/2 cup oil (corn oil is
 very good)
2 teaspoons vanilla

2 cups all purpose flour
1 teaspoon baking soda
2 teaspoons cinnamon
1 teaspoon salt
1 cup raisins
1 cup broken walnuts
 (leave in large pieces)

Preheat oven to 325°. Grease 16 muffin tins. Put 3 mixing bowls on the counter. Mix apples and sugar in one bowl and set aside. Put eggs, oil, and vanilla in second bowl and stir to blend well. In third bowl put flour, baking soda, cinnamon, and salt, and stir with a fork until blended. Stir egg mixture into apples and sugar, and mix thoroughly. Sprinkle flour mixture over apple mixture and mix well. Use your hands, as the batter is stiff. Sprinkle raisins and walnuts over batter and mix until they are evenly distributed. Spoon into muffin tins. Bake for 25 minutes and serve warm.

Submitted by Water's Edge B&B, Gig Harbor

Blueberry

♥ Lemon Yogurt Muffins ♥

2 1/4 cups flour
3/4 cup sugar
3/4 teaspoon baking powder
1/2 teaspoon baking soda
1/2 teaspoon salt

1/2 cup vegetable oil
3 tablespoons lemon juice
1 tablespoon grated lemon peel
1 egg
1 (8-ounce) carton lemon yogurt

1½ c. blueberries

In large bowl mix flour, sugar, baking powder, baking soda, and salt. In smaller bowl stir together vegetable oil, lemon juice, lemon peel, egg, and lemon yogurt. Gently fold yogurt mixture into dry ingredients. Spoon batter into 12 greased muffin tins. Bake at 375° for 20 minutes.

Submitted by The Guest House B&B, Seattle

♥ Lemon-Huckleberry Muffins ♥

3 1/2 cups flour
1 cup granulated sugar
2 teaspoons baking powder
1 teaspoon baking soda
1 teaspoon salt
1/2 cup flaked coconut
2 tablespoons lemon zest

1/2 cup wild huckleberries, or small blueberries
2 cups buttermilk
2 eggs
6 tablespoons canola oil or melted butter
1 teaspoon lemon oil or flavoring

Preheat oven to 400°. Measure first seven ingredients into one bowl. Add berries to dry ingredients and toss to coat with flour mixture. Make a well in the center. Mix all liquid ingredients and whisk together. Add liquids all at once to dry. Mix just until moist. Do not overmix or muffins will toughen. Spoon into muffin tins lined with paper cups. Muffin cups will be full, and pile batter high in the center. May spray paper cups with cooking spray so they don't stick to muffins. Bake for 20 minutes. Cool. Makes 12 large muffins.

Submitted by Eagles Nest Inn, Whidbey Island - Langley

♥   **Marnie's Marvelous Muffins**   ♥

2 1/4 cups mixed flour
(half unbleached white,
half whole wheat
pastry flour)
3/4 cup sugar
1 1/2 teaspoons baking
powder
1/2 teaspoon baking soda
Dash of salt

Dash of nutmeg
1 stick butter, melted
2 lightly beaten eggs
1 cup buttermilk
2 teaspoons vanilla (opt.)
1 1/2 cups frozen fruit
(try strawberries! - do
not thaw fruit)

Preheat oven to 400°. Combine first six ingredients in large bowl. In separate bowl combine melted butter, eggs, buttermilk, and vanilla if desired. Add wet ingredients to dry ingredients and mix only enough to moisten. Don't overmix. Then add fruit. Bake for 20 minutes in non-stick muffin pans or in greased muffin pans. Makes 12 large muffins.

Submitted by Angels of the Sea B&B, Vashon Island

♥   **Perfect Blueberry Muffins**   ♥

2 cups sifted all purpose
flour
1/3 cup sugar
3 teaspoons baking
powder
1/2 teaspoon salt
1/2 cup milk + 1/2
cup sour cream

1/3 cup salad oil
1 egg, slightly beaten
1 cup fresh blueberries
or 3/4 cup canned or
thawed commercial
frozen blueberries (if
using home frozen
blueberries, use 1 cup)

Preheat oven to 400°. Grease bottoms of muffin pans. Sift flour with sugar, baking powder and salt into large bowl. Make a well in center of flour mixture. Measure milk and sour cream into a 2-cup measure. Add oil and egg; beat with a fork to mix well. Pour milk mixture into well of flour mixture all at once. Stir quickly with fork, just until dry ingredients are moistened. Gently stir in blueberries. Do not beat, batter will be lumpy. Fill muffin cups slightly more than half full. Bake for 20 to 25 minutes or until golden and toothpick comes out clean. Serve hot. Makes 11 to 14 regular size muffins.

Submitted by The Rose of Gig Harbor, a B&B Inn, Gig Harbor

♥ Six Week Bran Muffins ♥

3 cups Bran Buds® cereal
3 cups All-Bran® cereal
2 cups boiling water
1 cup margarine
1 1/2 cups sugar
1 1/2 cups packed brown
   sugar
4 eggs

4 cups buttermilk
1/4 cup molasses
5 cups flour
2 tablespoons baking
   soda
1 tablespoon baking
   powder
1 teaspoon salt

In large bowl combine cereals and boiling water. Let stand. In mixing bowl cream margarine and sugars together. Add eggs one at a time beating after each addition. Mix in buttermilk. Add molasses. Stir in cereal mixture. In another bowl combine flour, baking soda, baking powder, and salt. Mix thoroughly. Add to batter. Stir just to combine. Store in refrigerator. Keeps for six weeks. When ready to bake fill muffin cups 3/4 full. Bake at 400° for 20 minutes. Variations: When ready to bake, add fresh raspberries or blueberries. Or fill each muffin cup half full of batter and put in 1 teaspoon of soft cream cheese, then top with more batter.

Submitted by Stratford Manor, Bellingham

♥ Skagit Berry Oatmeal Muffins ♥

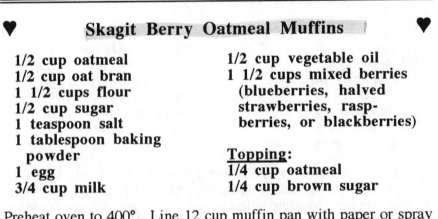

1/2 cup oatmeal
1/2 cup oat bran
1 1/2 cups flour
1/2 cup sugar
1 teaspoon salt
1 tablespoon baking
   powder
1 egg
3/4 cup milk

1/2 cup vegetable oil
1 1/2 cups mixed berries
   (blueberries, halved
   strawberries, rasp-
   berries, or blackberries)

Topping:
1/4 cup oatmeal
1/4 cup brown sugar

Preheat oven to 400°. Line 12 cup muffin pan with paper or spray with oil. Combine oatmeal, oat bran, flour, sugar, salt, and baking powder. Mix in egg, milk, and oil. Gently stir in berries just until mixed. Spoon batter into muffin pan. Mix together oatmeal and brown sugar for topping; sprinkle over batter. Bake for 17 to 20 minutes or until toothpick inserted in center comes out dry.

Submitted by White Swan Guest House, La Conner (Mt. Vernon)

♥ ## Texas "Pookie" Muffins ♥

1 cup white flour
1 cup whole wheat flour
2 teaspoons baking soda
1/2 teaspoon salt
2 teaspoons ground
    cinnamon
3 eggs, beaten
3/4 cup sugar

1/2 cup buttermilk
1 teaspoon vanilla
1/2 cup oil
1 1/2 cups grated carrots
1 1/2 cups grated apples
3/4 cup grated coconut
1/2 cup chopped dates
1/2 cup chopped walnuts

Sift together first five ingredients. Set aside. Beat eggs. Add sugar buttermilk, vanilla and oil to eggs and mix. Mix together last five ingredients and add half of the dry ingredients to this mixture. Add egg mixture and other half of dry ingredients. Stir until blended. Do not overmix. Spoon batter into greased muffin pan, or line with paper muffin cups. Bake at 375° for 15 to 18 minutes. Remove from the oven when they "spring back" and are golden brown. Let cool on wire rack for a few minutes before serving. Makes 24 muffins. They freeze well. ("Pookie" is a term of endearment for children in Texas, where I lived and raised my family of six children.)

Submitted by Highland Inn of San Juan Island, Friday Harbor

♥ ## Washington State Apple Muffins ♥

2 cups sugar
1/2 cup vegetable oil
2 eggs
2 teaspoons vanilla
2 cups flour

2 teaspoons baking
    soda
2 teaspoons cinnamon
1 teaspoon salt (opt.)
4 cups chopped apple

In large bowl beat sugar, vegetable oil, eggs and vanilla. Slowly stir in dry ingredients just until flour is moistened. Fold in chopped apple. Fill greased muffin tins 2/3 full. Bake at 400° for approximately 20 minutes. Makes 8 muffins.

Submitted by The Guest House B&B, Seattle

♥ ## White Swan Blackberry Muffins ♥

1/2 cup (1 stick) butter,
  softened
1 1/4 cups sugar
2 eggs, room temperature
2 cups flour
2 teaspoons baking
  powder

1/2 teaspoon salt
1/2 cup milk
2 cups fresh (or frozen)
  blackberries
4 teaspoons sugar

Preheat oven to 375°. Grease 18 - 1/2 cup muffin cups (or use paper liners). Using electric mixer, cream butter and sugar in large bowl until light. Add eggs, one at a time, beating well after each addition. Sift flour, baking powder, and salt into small bowl. Mix dry ingredients into butter mixture, alternately with milk. Fold in berries. Divide batter among prepared cups. Sprinkle tops evenly with sugar. Bake about 20 minutes until tester inserted comes out clean.

Submitted by White Swan Guest House, La Conner (Mt. Vernon)

♥ ## Blueberry Scones ♥

2 cups flour
1/4 cup sugar
1 tablespoon baking
  powder
1 tablespoon finely
  shredded orange peel
1/4 teaspoon salt
1/4 teaspoon baking soda

1/4 cup butter
1 egg or 1/4 cup egg
  product
2/3 cup buttermilk
1 teaspoon vanilla
1 cup fresh or frozen
  blueberries (or fresh
  cranberries)

Stir together flour, sugar, baking powder, orange peel, salt and baking soda. Cut in butter until mixture resembles coarse crumbs. Make a well in center of dry ingredients. Stir together egg, buttermilk and vanilla. Add to flour mixture. Stir with a fork until just moistened. Carefully stir in blueberries. Turn onto lightly floured board and knead lightly. Pat dough into an approximately 7" circle on baking sheet. Cut dough into 8 wedges. (I separate wedges slightly so they bake more evenly.) Bake at 400° for 15 to 20 minutes. Serve warm. These are also very tasty with just the orange zest or with the fresh cranberries.

Submitted by Stratford Manor, Bellingham

♥ Cranberry & White Chocolate Scones ♥

1 3/4 cups all purpose
   flour
1/4 cup sugar
2 1/2 teaspoons baking
   powder
1/2 teaspoon salt
5 tablespoons chilled,
   unsalted butter, cut
   into pieces

6 tablespoons half &
   half milk
1 large egg, beaten
1/2 cup cranberries,
   fresh, frozen, or
   dried
1/2 cup white chocolate
   chips

Blend flour, sugar, baking powder, salt, and butter. Add milk, egg, cranberries, and white chocolate chips. Stir until dough begins to hold together. Turn onto lightly floured board. Knead for 2 minutes. Pat into 1/2" round; cut into 8 wedges. Transfer to baking sheet sprayed with vegetable oil. Bake at 400° for 14 minutes until golden brown.

Submitted by Inn at Barnum Point, Camano Island

♥ Date-Nut Scones ♥

2 cups flour
1/4 cup brown sugar
2 teaspoons baking
   powder
1/2 teaspoon baking soda
1/2 teaspoon salt
1/4 cup butter

1 cup vanilla yogurt
1 egg yolk, beaten
1/2 cup chopped
   walnuts
1/2 cup chopped dates
1 egg white, slightly
   beaten

In large mixing bowl stir together flour, brown sugar, baking powder, baking soda, and salt. Using pastry blender, cut in butter until mixture resembles coarse crumbs. Make a well in center. In small mixing bowl stir together yogurt, egg yolk, walnuts, and dates; add all at once to flour mixture. Stir with fork until combined. Turn dough onto lightly floured surface. Quickly knead dough using 10 to 12 strokes or until nearly smooth. Pat lightly into 7" circle. Cut into 8 wedges. Arrange on ungreased baking sheet about 1" apart. Brush with egg white. Bake at 400° for 10 to 12 minutes until lightly brown.

Submitted by Albatross B&B, Anacortes

♥ # Gingerbread Scones ♥

1/3 cup milk
1/3 cup light molasses
2 cups all purpose flour
2 teaspoons baking
  powder
1/4 teaspoon baking soda
1 teaspoon ground
  cinnamon

1 teaspoon ground
  ginger
1/4 teaspoon ground
  cloves
Dash of nutmeg
7 tablespoons cold,
  unsalted butter, cut
  into pieces

Preheat oven to 425°. Measure milk in glass measuring cup; add molasses to 2/3 cup mark and stir to blend. Mix dry ingredients in large bowl. Add butter and cut in with pastry blender or rub with your fingers until mixture looks like fine granules. Stir milk mixture and add to flour. Blend with a fork to firm, smooth dough. Turn out dough onto lightly floured surface, knead 10 to 12 times. Cut dough in half. Knead each half into a ball, turn smooth side up, and place on ungreased cookie sheet. Pat each piece of dough into 5" circle, cut into 6 or 8 wedges, leaving sides touching. Bake about 10 minutes or until medium brown. Cool, loosely covered with cloth, on wire rack. Serve warm. These freeze nicely.

Submitted by Boreas B&B Inn, Long Beach

♥ # Grill-Baked Scotch Scones ♥

6 cups biscuit mix
3/4 cup sugar

2 eggs
1 1/2 cups milk

Preheat grill to 300° - 325°. Stir together biscuit mix and sugar. Make well in center. Place eggs and milk in well. Lightly whip eggs and milk with a knife, then stir into dry ingredients just until combined. Mixture should be softer than biscuit dough. Turn onto heavily floured pastry sheet. Turn, pat to 3/4" thick. Cut into 2 1/2" - 3" squares. Bake on grill for around 30 minutes, turning once when golden. Serve with butter and jam or honey.

Submitted by Buck Bay Farm, Orcas Island

♥ Lemon Cream Scones ♥

2 cups unbleached flour
2 tablespoons sugar
1 teaspoon cream of
   tartar
1/2 teaspoon baking
   soda
1/2 teaspoon salt
Grated zest of 2
   lemons

4 tablespoons unsalted
   butter, cut into pieces
2 eggs
1/2 cup heavy cream
Cinnamon-sugar mixture
   (1/2 teaspoon cinnamon
   mixed with 2 table-
   spoons sugar) for
   sprinkling (opt.)

Preheat oven to 400°. Combine flour, sugar, cream of tartar, baking soda, salt and lemon zest and blend. This can be blended in the workbowl of a food processor. With pastry blender, 2 knives or steel blade of a food processor, cut or process butter in until mixture resembles coarse meal. Whisk together eggs and heavy cream. Add to dry mixture and stir until sticky dough is formed. If using a food processor, pour mixture in feed tube and pulse until dough starts to form a rough ball (don't overprocess or scones will be tough). Turn dough out onto lightly floured work surface and knead gently just until dough holds together, about 6 times. Pat out dough into an 8" to 10" round and with a knife, cut into 8 wedges (a biscuit cutter can also be used). Remember that, as with biscuits, you stamp or punch and not slice. Place scones about 1" apart on a greased or parchment-lined baking sheet. Sprinkle with cinnamon-sugar mixture, if desired. Bake until crusty and golden brown about 15 to 20 minutes. Serve hot with butter and jam, or homemade Devonshire cream.

Submitted by The Whalebone House,
Ocean Park - Long Beach Peninsula

www.wbbg.com

♥ Lemon-Walnut Scones ♥

1/3 cup butter	3 cups all purpose flour,
1/3 cup margarine	sifted
1 tablespoon baking	1 egg
powder	1 teaspoon vanilla extract
1/8 teaspoon salt	1 cup milk
2/3 cup sugar	1/3 cup chopped walnuts
1 grated lemon peel	Extra flour

Cut butter, margarine, baking powder, salt, sugar, and lemon peel together in large bowl. Cut 3 cups sifted flour into above ingredients until crumbly. Mix egg, vanilla, and milk together and add to above ingredients. Add walnuts and mix well. Ingredients should be loose enough to mix with spoon; add more milk if necessary. Scoop heaping tablespoon portions into a bowl of flour, and roll until covered. Place on cookie sheet. Bake at 400° for 20 minutes, until done. Makes 24 scones.

Submitted by Hillside House B&B, San Juan Island

♥ Nantucket Inn's Raspberry Scones ♥

2 1/2 cups any scone mix	Half & half, to taste
1/2 cup sugar	2 eggs, beaten
1/2 stick butter	Raspberries
2 eggs, beaten	Flour & sugar mixture

Mix together scone mix and sugar. Cut butter into 4 chunks and add to beaten eggs. Fold into scone mix and sugar along with half & half. Knead dough until gluten holds it together. Divide into 4 equal portions. Flatten each portion to 3/4" thick on lightly floured board. Make finger prints in dough 1/2" apart. Place a raspberry in each finger print. Fold dough portions together and make dome with berries inside. Cut into quarters again. Mix small amount of flour and sugar together and dip cut edge of scones to seal. Place on buttered baking air pan and bake at 425° for 10 minutes. Take out, cover with tin foil and bake for another 7 - 10 minutes. Makes 16 scones.

Submitted by Nantucket Inn, Anacortes

♥ # Oatmeal Scones ♥

1/2 cup butter
1 1/4 cups flour
1/2 cup sugar
1/2 teaspoon baking soda
1/2 teaspoon salt

1 teaspoon baking
  powder
1 cup buckeye old-
  fashioned oats
1/3 cup lemon yogurt

Blend butter, flour, sugar, baking soda, salt, and baking powder in food processor until well mixed. Add oats. Add yogurt and knead until you can pat into a 7" round. Cut into 8 wedges; transfer to ungreased baking sheet. Bake at 375° for 17 minutes. Note: Ingredients without yogurt can be refrigerated overnight. In morning add yogurt, prepare, and bake.

Submitted by Ravenscroft Inn, Port Townsend

 # Olympic Lights Blueberry Scones ♥

2 cups flour
2 tablespoons sugar
2 teaspoons baking
  powder
1/2 teaspoon baking
  soda

1/2 teaspoon salt
6 tablespoons cold butter
1/2 cup frozen blueberries
2 eggs
1/2 cup buttermilk
Sugar for tops

In large bowl sift together first five ingredients. Cut in cold butter. Stir in blueberries. In small bowl beat together eggs and buttermilk. Combine dry and wet ingredients, mixing as little as possible. (I use a very large bowl so that I can toss the ingredients together.) Turn dough onto floured surface. Pat into 1/2" thick round and cut into 12 scones. Brush with more buttermilk and sprinkle with sugar. Place on ungreased cookie sheet. Bake in top third of oven at 450° for 12 minutes.

Submitted by Olympic Lights, San Juan Island

♥ Orange Scones ♥

2 cups flour	1/4 cup dried cranberries
2 tablespoons sugar	(or dried currants)
1 tablespoon baking	1 tablespoon finely
powder	grated orange rind
1/2 teaspoon salt	6 tablespoons butter
1/4 cup diced candied	1 egg, lightly beaten
ginger	1/2 cup milk

In large bowl combine flour, sugar, baking powder and salt. Stir in ginger, cranberries and orange rind. Cut in butter until crumbly. Add egg and milk. Stir until dough clings together. Knead gently on a lightly floured board. Cut dough into fourths and form squares about 1/2" thick. Cut each square diagonally twice to form 4 triangles. Bake on ungreased baking sheet at 400° for 11 to 15 minutes. Makes 16 scones. Note: Dough can be frozen for future baking.

Submitted by The Farm, a B&B, Trout Lake

www.wbbg.com

Breads ~ Pastries

Melissa Pigg ©

Napkin Folding

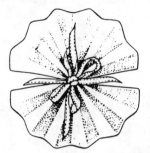

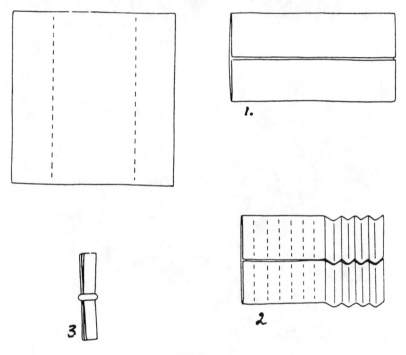

Wheel

1. Fold the top and bottom edges of the napkin to the center.
2. Pleat the rectangle into one-inch pleats.
3. Tie a ribbon around the center of the napkin. Fan out the pleats to make a wheel shape.

♥ **Apricot Bran Bread** ♥

Boiling water
1 cup finely snipped dried
  apricots
3 tablespoons sugar
1 1/2 cups sifted all-
  purpose flour
1/2 cup sugar
3 3/4 teaspoons baking
  powder

1 teaspoon salt
1 1/2 cups whole bran
  cereal
1 cup milk
2 beaten eggs
1/3 cup cooking oil
Nuts, to taste (walnuts or
  pecans, chopped)
Sugar for top

Pour enough boiling water over dried apricots to cover; let stand 10 minutes. Drain well; combine apricots and 3 tablespoons sugar. Sift together flour, 1/2 cup sugar, baking powder, and salt. Mix bran cereal, milk, eggs, and oil. Add to flour mixture, stirring just until moistened. Gently stir in apricot mixture; add nuts, and turn into greased 9" x 5" x 3" loaf pan. Sprinkle top with a little sugar. Bake at 350° for one hour. Note: This is even better made the day before it is to be served.

Submitted by Water's Edge B&B, Gig Harbor

♥ **Blueberry-Lemon Yogurt Bread** ♥

2 tablespoons softened
  butter
1 egg
1 cup sugar
1 (8-ounce) carton lemon
  lowfat yogurt
2 cups flour

1 teaspoon baking
  powder
1/2 teaspoon baking
  soda
1/2 teaspoon salt
1 cup fresh or frozen
  blueberries

Preheat oven to 350°. In large bowl, combine butter, egg, sugar, and lemon yogurt. Mix well. In separate bowl, mix flour, baking powder, baking soda, and salt. Add flour mixture to yogurt mixture, and mix just until moistened. Fold in blueberries. Pour batter into greased 9" x 5" loaf pan. Bake for 45 to 60 minutes, until bread tests done. Makes 1 large, delicious loaf.

Submitted by White Swan Guest House, La Conner (Mt. Vernon)

♥ Cranberry Bread ♥

2 cups sifted flour
2/3 cup sugar
1 1/2 teaspoons baking
  powder
1/2 teaspoon salt
Juice and grated rind of
  1 orange

2 tablespoons melted
  shortening
Water, as needed
1 egg, well-beaten
2 cups cranberries, cut
  in half, or chopped
1/2 cup chopped nuts

Sift dry ingredients together. Combine orange juice, rind, melted shortening, and enough water to make 3/4 cup juice. Then stir in egg. Pour this mixture into dry ingredients, mixing just enough to moisten. Fold in cranberries and nuts. Bake in 9" x 5" x 3" pan or two loaf pans at 350° for 45 to 60 minutes. Remove from pan and cool. Store overnight for easy slicing. Can be frozen.

Submitted by Water's Edge B&B, Gig Harbor

♥ Cranberry Pudding Bread ♥

1 cup white
  sugar
2 cups flour
2 1/2 teaspoons baking
  powder

5 tablespoons melted
  butter
1 cup milk
3 cups fresh frozen whole
  cranberries (12 ounces)

Mix together dry ingredients and set aside. Keep cranberries frozen until ready to mix into batter. Melt butter. Stir milk into dry ingredients. Next, stir in melted butter. Last, stir in frozen cranberries. Spread batter in 1 greased regular-sized loaf bread pan or 2 smaller greased pans. Bake in preheated 350° oven for about 50 to 60 minutes for large pan or less time for smaller pans. Knife inserted into bread should come out clean. Cool for about 15 minutes and then turn out. This is a sweet and sour bread.

Submitted by The FARMHOUSE,Whidbey Island - Langley

♥ # Island Mango Bread ♥

2 cups flour
2 teaspoons baking soda
1 teaspoon cinnamon
1/2 teaspoon salt
1 cup sugar
3 eggs, beaten
1 cup salad oil

2 cups finely diced
  mangoes
2 teaspoons lemon
  juice
1/2 cup chopped nuts
1/2 cup raisins or
  coconut

Peel and dice mangoes. Add lemon juice and set aside. Sift dry ingredients together. Combine eggs with oil, mangoes, and lemon juice. Add nuts, raisins or coconut, and then dry mixture; mix well. Pour into greased and floured (I use fine cracker crumbs) loaf pans. Bake at 350° for 50 to 60 minutes. I slice and serve with French imported butter which I press into molds and freeze a day ahead, then soften to room temperature before serving. Makes 4 mini loaves.

Submitted by Island Escape B&B, Gig Harbor Area

♥ # Lemon Bread ♥

1/2 cup margarine,
  softened
1 cup sugar
2 eggs
1/4 cup milk
1/4 cup lemon yogurt
1 1/2 cups flour
1/2 teaspoon salt

1 teaspoon baking
  powder
Grated rind of 1 large
  or 2 small lemons
Glaze:
2 - 3 tablespoons lemon
  juice
1/2 cup sugar

Preheat oven to 350°. Spray 9" x 5" loaf pan with Pam®. Cream margarine and 1 cup sugar; add eggs one at a time. Add milk, yogurt, flour, salt, baking powder, and lemon rind. Mix well. Pour into loaf pan. Bake at 350° for one hour. Mix lemon juice with 1/2 cup sugar and spoon over bread immediately upon removal from oven. Let cool in pan.

Submitted by Reflections B&B, Port Orchard

♥ ## Lemon Poppy Seed Bread ♥

1 box white cake mix without pudding	4 eggs
1 (3.4-ounce) box instant lemon pudding mix	1 cup warm water
	1/2 cup vegetable oil
	4 teaspoons poppy seeds

In mixing bowl combine cake and pudding mixes, eggs, water, and oil. Beat until well mixed. Fold in poppy seeds. Pour into 2 greased 9" x 5" x 3" loaf pans. Bake at 350° for 35 to 40 minutes or until bread tests done. Cool in pans for 10 minutes before removing to wire rack. Can be topped with a powdered sugar glaze.

Submitted by Marianna Stoltz House B&B, Spokane

♥ ## Orange Bread With Blueberry Sauce ♥

2 eggs, beaten	2 tablespoons baking powder
1/2 cup vegetable oil	1 large orange, unpeeled
4 cups all purpose flour, unsifted	1 1/2 cups milk
1 2/3 cups sugar	Butter and flour for preparing pans
1/2 teaspoon salt	

Blueberry Sauce:

2 pints blueberries, sorted and cleaned	1/2 cup sugar
	1/2 cup maple syrup

Preheat oven to 400°. Beat eggs until thick and gradually add oil. Beat for one minute. Sift dry ingredients together and add to egg mixture. Cut orange into pieces and chop finely in food processor. Add to batter. Slowly beat in milk and continue beating for 2 minutes. Turn out into 2 (8" x 5") loaf pans that have been buttered and floured. Let stand for 20 minutes. Bake for 20 minutes or until dough has risen to top of pan and started to brown slightly. Reduce oven temperature to 300° and score top of bread lengthwise with point of knife. Bake for 40 minutes longer or until toothpick inserted in center comes out clean. Allow to stand in pans for 10 minutes before turning out onto a rack to cool. This bread can be served sliced with orange butter or orange-pineapple cream cheese. It is also excellent as French Toast. Slice and dip in egg-milk mixture and brown on griddle brushed with butter. Serve French Toast with Blueberry Sauce: Combine all ingredients in saucepan and cook over medium heat until blueberries are soft.

Submitted by Villa Heidelberg, Seattle

♥ **Pear Bread** ♥

2 cups sugar
3 eggs, well beaten
1 teaspoon vanilla
1 1/2 cups oil
3 cups flour

1 teaspoon baking
 soda
2 teaspoons cinnamon
1 teaspoon salt
3 cups chopped pears

Preheat oven to 350°. Grease 2 (9") loaf pans. In a large bowl combine sugar, eggs, vanilla and oil. Beat well. In a separate bowl combine flour, baking soda, cinnamon and salt. Add to sugar mixture one cup at a time, mixing well after each addition. Fold in pears. Pour into prepared pans and bake for 1 hour. This is excellent. Serve the next day after baking.

Submitted by English Tudor View, Seattle

♥ **Sour Cream Banana Bread** ♥

3/4 cup margarine
2 1/2 cups sugar
3 eggs
1 1/2 cups mashed
 bananas
6 tablespoons sour
 cream

3 cups flour
1 1/2 teaspoons baking
 soda
1/2 teaspoon salt
2 teaspoons vanilla
1 cup chopped walnuts
 (opt.)

Cream margarine and sugar with mixer, and beat in eggs. Mash bananas (3 average bananas yield 1 1/2 cups mashed bananas) and add to batter. Beat in sour cream, flour, baking soda, salt, and vanilla. Fold in nuts if desired. Pour batter into 2 well greased bread pans. Bake at 400° for 1 1/2 hours. Watch closely to see they don't overcook and dry out.

Submitted by Katy's Inn, La Conner

♥ Whole Wheat Banana Walnut Bread ♥

8 medium, ripe bananas
3/4 pound butter
1 1/2 cups sugar
1 1/2 cups brown sugar
4 eggs
1 cup buttermilk
2 cups whole wheat flour

2 cups white flour
2 teaspoons salt
2 teaspoons baking
soda
1 tablespoon maple
extract
2 cups chopped walnuts

Mix bananas, butter, sugars, eggs, buttermilk, flours, salt, baking soda, maple extract, and walnuts in large mixing bowl until well blended. Pour into 2 - 3 sprayed bread pans. Bake at 325° for one hour. Check the center and bake until toothpick comes out clean.

Submitted by The Orcas Hotel, Orcas Island

♥ Apple Almond Tart ♥

1 large egg, beaten
1 tablespoon water
1 (7-ounce) jar Odense®
pure almond paste
2 teaspoons vanilla
3 medium apples, thinly
sliced (Braeburn, Fugi
or Jonagold)

2 teaspoons flour
1 (17 1/2-ounce) pkg.
Pepperidge Farm®
frozen puff pastry
sheets, thawed
2 teaspoons sugar mixed
with 1/4 teaspoon
cinnamon

In small bowl beat egg. Remove 1 tablespoon egg and put into measuring cup with water. Add almond paste and vanilla to the egg in the bowl, and blend well. In medium bowl gently toss apple slices with flour. Unfold one pastry sheet on lightly floured surface; roll out to a 13" square. Trim to make a circle and transfer to cookie sheet. Spread almond paste mixture up to 1" from edge. Arrange apple slices in concentric rings on filling, slightly overlapping slices. Unfold second sheet of pastry, roll and trim as with first sheet. Brush egg/water mixture along the 1" edge of first pastry and cover with second sheet; crimp edges to seal. Cut slits in top for decoration and steam vents. Brush remaining egg/water mixture over top, sprinkle with sugar/cinnamon mixture. (Can be prepared to this point, then covered and refrigerated for up to 4 hours before baking.) Bake at 375° for 25 to 30 minutes until golden. Cool for 10 - 15 minutes before serving. Serve with whipped cream and/or ice cream. Makes 12 servings.

Submitted by Soundview B&B, Seattle

♥ Baked Apple Pinwheel ♥

2 (8-count) tubes
  crescent rolls
2 medium apples, peeled
  & finely chopped
2/3 cup raisins
1/4 cup sugar

1 teaspoon grated
  lemon rind
Nutmeg, to taste
Milk
2 tablespoons light
  brown sugar

Preheat oven to 350°. Separate dough into triangles. Arrange triangles in circle on baking sheet with points out, overlapping corners of wide edges slightly to form center of circle. Press overlapping edges to seal. Combine apples, raisins, sugar, lemon rind, and nutmeg in medium bowl; mix well. Spoon into ring toward center of pinwheel. Fold points of dough over filling and secure under center edge of circle. Brush with milk; sprinkle with brown sugar. Bake for 25 minutes or until golden brown. For a festive touch, drizzle a little powdered sugar glaze over top and decorate with candied cherries and pecans. Makes 12 servings.

Submitted by Commencement Bay B&B, Tacoma

♥ Blueberry Bundt Coffee Cake ♥

1/2 cup butter
3/4 cup sugar
2 eggs
1 teaspoon vanilla
1/4 teaspoon salt

2 cups flour
1 teaspoon baking powder
1 teaspoon baking soda
1 cup sour cream
1 1/2 cups blueberries

Topping:
2 tablespoons melted
  butter
1/2 cup brown sugar

1 tablespoon cinnamon
2 tablespoons flour
1/2 cup chopped nuts

Combine first four ingredients. Beat well after each addition. Combine dry ingredients and stir into wet mixture. Stir in sour cream and blueberries. For Topping: Mix melted butter, brown sugar, cinnamon, and flour with pastry cutter; then stir in nuts. Spread half of batter into greased bundt pan. Spoon on topping mixture, and cover with remaining batter. Bake at 350° for 40 to 50 minutes. Cool for 5 minutes in pan, then turn out onto serving plate. Makes 12 - 14 servings.

Submitted by The Meadows B&B, San Juan Island - Friday Harbor

♥ Caramel Pecan Sticky Rolls ♥

Caramel Sauce:
1/2 cup packed brown
  sugar
1/2 cup light corn syrup

4 tablespoons butter
1 cup pecan pieces or
  halves

Dough:
6 - 7 cups flour,
  divided
1/3 cup granulated sugar
2 pkgs. quick-rise yeast
1 1/2 teaspoons salt
3/4 cup warm water
  (110° - 115°)

3/4 cup warm milk
1/3 cup melted butter
2 eggs

Melted butter and
  cinnamon, to taste,
  for filling

For Caramel Sauce: In small saucepan heat together brown sugar, corn syrup and butter. Cook briefly only until the 3 ingredients are well blended together. Do not cook any longer as this will bake with the rolls later. Pour caramel into a 9" x 13" pan, spreading evenly over the bottom. Arrange pecans evenly over caramel. Roll Dough: In large bowl combine 2 cups flour, sugar, yeast and salt. Stir in warm water, warm milk, 1/3 cup melted butter and eggs. When this is well blended, stir in 4 to 5 more cups of flour. Knead on well-floured surface until smooth and elastic, for about 5 to 8 minutes. Roll dough out into an 18" x 24" rectangle. Brush dough with melted butter, then sprinkle with cinnamon, to taste. Begin at the short end of the rectangle and roll up as you would a jelly roll. Pinch the seams to seal. Cut into 10 rolls with a sharp knife. Place rolls on caramel in the pan, cut sides up. At this time you can choose to set in a warm draft-free place to rise for at least 20 to 40 minutes. Then bake at 375° for 30 minutes. Let cool in pan for no more than 10 minutes, then turn out onto a cookie sheet. Let the pan remain on the rolls for another 5 minutes, then remove pan. Note: You may also choose to cover the rolls tightly with plastic wrap and refrigerate for 2 to 24 hours before they are baked. Remove from refrigerator, uncover dough and let rise in a warm place for 45 minutes, then bake as directed. Makes 10 rolls.

Submitted by Edenwild Inn, Lopez Island

♥ ## Citrus Coffee Buns ♥

Batter:
1 pkg. active dry yeast
1 cup warm milk (105° - 115°)
3/4 cup sugar
1/2 cup butter, softened
1/2 teaspoon salt
2 large eggs
3 1/2 - 4 cups flour

Filling:
1/2 cup butter, softened
1/2 cup sugar
1 large egg
2 tablespoons lime juice
1 teaspoon grated lime peel
1 egg, lightly beaten, for glaze

For Batter: Dissolve yeast in warm milk in large bowl for 5 to 10 minutes. Mix 3/4 cup sugar, 1/2 cup softened butter, and salt into yeast mixture. Beat in 2 eggs, one at a time, then add flour 1/2 cup at a time until a soft dough forms. On floured surface, knead dough until smooth and elastic, 5 to 10 minutes. Add more flour to prevent sticking. Place dough in large greased bowl, turning to coat. Cover, let rise in warm place for one hour. For Filling: Beat 1/2 cup softened butter and 1/2 cup sugar together until light and fluffy. Beat in egg, lime juice, and lime peel. Grease 2 baking sheets. Punch down dough. On floured surface with floured rolling pin roll into 20" x 12" rectangle. Spread filling evenly to within 1/2" of edges. Starting with long side, roll up jelly roll style. Cut into 16 pieces. Using a chopstick or handle of wooden spoon, press vertical line down the center of each bun. Place buns 2" apart on baking sheets. Cover and let rise in warm place for 30 minutes. Heat oven to 400°. Brush with beaten egg. Bake for 15 minutes until golden. Transfer to wire rack to cool. Makes 16 buns.

Submitted by Soundview B&B, Seattle

www.wbbg.com

♥ Coffee Cake With Cinnamon Walnut Topping ♥

1 box yellow cake mix,
  with pudding in the mix
1 stick margarine or
  butter, melted

4 whole eggs
1/4 cup oil
1 1/2 cups sour
  cream

Cinnamon Walnut Topping:
1 1/4 cups brown
  sugar

1 tablespoon cinnamon
1 1/4 cups chopped nuts

Mix cake mix, margarine, eggs, oil and sour cream all together. Batter will be thick, don't overmix. Mix topping ingredients together. Grease 9" x 13" pan or 2 square glass pans. Pour in batter, then top with Cinnamon Walnut Topping. Swirl topping into batter with tip of knife. Bake at 350° for 40 to 45 minutes. This freezes well and is good served warm or cold.

Submitted by Otters Pond B&B of Orcas Island, Orcas Island

♥ Fruit Kuchens ♥

Dough:
1 teaspoon baking powder
1/2 teaspoon salt
1 1/4 cups flour

1/4 cup sugar
2 tablespoons butter
1 egg plus milk to
  make 1/2 cup liquid

Filling:
Sliced fruit (apple, peach,
  raspberry, cherry
  or plum, etc.)

1 cup sugar
4 tablespoons flour
Sprinkle of cinnamon

For dough: Mix dry ingredients; add butter. In separate bowl beat egg slightly and add milk. Combine 2 mixtures. Roll or pat dough 1/4" thick in coffee cake tin. For apple, peach or raspberry: Place sliced fruit in rows on dough. Cover with mixture of sugar, flour and cinnamon. (Or use this custard variation: Beat 1 egg, 1/2 cup sugar and 2 tablespoons cream. Pour over fruit and sprinkle with cinnamon.) Bake at 350° for 15 minutes. Reduce temperature to 325° and bake for another 15 minutes. For cherry or plum: Use same recipe, but use 1 1/2 cups sugar in fruit filling.

Submitted by 1908 Cooney Mansion, Aberdeen (Cosmopolis)

♥ ## Grandma's Peach Kuchen ♥

1/2 cup butter, softened
1/4 cup sugar
1 teaspoon vanilla
1 egg
1 cup all purpose flour
1/2 teaspoon baking
 powder

1/4 teaspoon salt
1 (29-ounce) can sliced
 peaches, drained
3 tablespoons sugar
1 teaspoon cinnamon

Custard: (opt.)
1 egg

2 tablespoons milk or
 half and half

Heat oven to 350°. Grease 9" springform pan. In large bowl beat butter and sugar until light and fluffy. Add vanilla and egg; beat well. Add flour, baking powder and salt to butter mixture; blend well. Spread dough over bottom and 1" up sides of pan. Arrange peach slices in "spoke" fashion over dough. Sprinkle with sugar and cinnamon. Mix egg with milk or half and half for custard. Pour over peaches. Bake for 30 to 35 minutes or until edges are golden brown. Cool for 10 minutes; remove sides of pan. Makes 8 - 10 servings. Note: Italian prunes are a traditional favorite for kuchens.

Submitted by Boreas B&B Inn, Long Beach

♥ ## Gran's Cinnamon Coffee Cake ♥

3 cups unbleached white
 flour
2 1/2 teaspoons baking
 powder
3/4 teaspoon baking soda
3/4 teaspoon salt
6 tablespoons melted
 butter

1 1/2 cups sugar
2 eggs
1 1/2 cups buttermilk
Dark brown sugar,
 to taste
Cinnamon, to taste
1 cup chopped nuts
2 tablespoons butter

Whisk dry ingredients together. Cream melted butter, sugar, and eggs. Add dry ingredients and buttermilk alternately, stirring well. Spread in greased or sprayed 9" x 13" pan. Cover well with brown sugar, sprinkle on lots of cinnamon; add nuts, and dot with 2 tablespoons butter. Bake at 350° for about 35 minutes.

Submitted by The Meadows B&B, San Juan Island - Friday Harbor

♥ Hummingbird Inn Fresh Pear Coffee Cake ♥

3/4 cup sugar
1/4 cup softened
  margarine
1 teaspoon vanilla
3 egg whites or 1/2 cup
  egg substitute
1 3/4 cups all purpose
  flour
1 teaspoon baking powder

1/2 teaspoon baking
  soda
1/2 teaspoon ground
  cardamom
1/4 teaspoon salt
1 cup reduced fat sour
  cream
2 cups unpeeled pears,
  chopped

Streusel Topping:
1/3 cup granulated sugar
1/3 cup brown sugar
2 tablesoons flour
1/2 teaspoon cinnamon

Chopped nuts, to taste
  (opt.)
2 tablespoons firm
  margarine or butter

Preheat oven to 350°. Spray 9" x 13" pan with non stick spray. Beat sugar and margarine, vanilla and egg whites in large bowl on medium speed for 2 minutes. Mix flour, baking powder, baking soda, cardamom and salt. Beat dry mixture into sugar mixture in small amounts, alternating with sour cream, on slow speed. Fold in pears. Pour batter into prepared pan. Sprinkle with Streusel: Mix together dry ingredients. Cut in margarine or butter until crumbly. Bake for 45 to 55 minutes or until toothpick inserted in the center comes out clean. Cool. Makes 15 - 16 servings.

Submitted by Hummingbird Inn, Roslyn

www.wbbg.com

♥ ## Jerry's Soon To Be World-Famous Sticky Buns ♥

4 - 4 1/2 cups all
   purpose flour
1 tablespoon dry yeast
1 cup milk
1/3 cup sugar

1/3 cup butter
1 teaspoon salt
2 eggs
4 tablespoons butter

Sauce Ingredients:
2/3 cup packed brown
   sugar
1/4 cup butter
2 tablespoons dark
   corn syrup
Chopped pecans, to taste

Filling Ingredients:
1/2 cup granulated
   sugar
2 teaspoons ground
   cinnamon
Raisins, to taste

In mixer bowl combine 2 cups flour and yeast. Heat milk, 1/3 cup sugar, 1/3 cup butter and salt until warm (115° - 120°); stir constantly. Add to flour mixture; add eggs. Beat with mixer at low speed for 1/2 minute. Then beat at high speed for 3 minutes. Stir in as much of the remaining flour as you can mix in with a spoon. On a floured surface, knead in enough of the remaining flour to make a moderately stiff dough that is smooth and elastic, for about 6 to 8 minutes. Shape into a ball and place in a greased bowl. Cover and let rise in warm place until double, for about 1 hour. Punch down, divide in half. Cover and let rest for 10 minutes. While dough is resting, combine brown sugar, butter and dark corn syrup in saucepan to make sauce. Cook and stir until blended. Divide between 2 - 9" round or square baking pans. Sprinkle a liberal amount of chopped pecans on each pan. Melt 4 tablespoons butter. Roll out one piece of the dough into a 12" x 8" rectangle. Brush with half the melted butter. Combine 1/2 cup granulated sugar and 2 teaspoons ground cinnamon. sprinkle half the cinnamon-sugar over the dough. Sprinkle with raisins, to taste. Roll up jelly roll style, beginning from the longest side, tucking in ends. Cut into 9 - 12 pieces and place in pan. Repeat with second piece of dough. Cover and let rise until double for about 45 minutes. Bake at 375° for 15 to 17 minutes. Remove from oven and invert on serving plate immediately. Be sure to scrape all the nuts and caramel from bottom of pan. ENJOY!

Submitted by Apple Country B&B, Wenatchee

♥ **Oatmeal Coffee Cake** ♥

1 cup quick oatmeal
1 1/4 cups boiling water
1 stick margarine, melted
1 cup sugar
1 cup brown sugar

2 eggs
1 teaspoon vanilla
1 1/3 cups flour
1 teaspoon baking soda
1 teaspoon salt

Topping:
1/2 stick butter, melted
1/4 teaspoon vanilla
1 cup brown sugar

1/2 cup evaporated
  milk
1 cup coconut

Pour boiling water over oats and let cool. Cream together 1 stick melted margarine, sugar, brown sugar, eggs, and 1 teaspoon vanilla. Add cooled oatmeal and mix well. Add flour, baking soda, and salt, and beat well. Pour into greased 9" x 13" pan and bake at 350° for 35 minutes. Remove from oven. For Topping: Melt butter; mix in vanilla, brown sugar, evaporated milk, and coconut. Spread over cake. Put under broiler to brown, watching carefully. Remove from oven, cool, cut, and serve. Makes 16 servings.

Submitted by The Duffy House B&B, Friday Harbor

♥ **Pear/Walnut Breakfast Cake** ♥

Topping:
1 1/2 cups chopped
  walnuts
1/2 cup brown sugar

1/2 cup flour
1/4 cup chopped butter
1 1/2 teaspoons cinnamon

Cake Batter:
1/2 cup softened butter
1 cup sugar
1 teaspoon vanilla
3 eggs
2 cups flour
1 teaspoon baking powder

1 teaspoon baking soda
1/4 teaspoon salt
1 1/4 cups sour cream
2 fresh pears, sliced or
  well-drained, firm,
  canned pears

Mix together topping ingredients and set aside. For batter: Cream butter, sugar and vanilla. Add eggs. Add dry ingredients, alternating with sour cream. Prepare pears. Grease and flour a 9" - 10" springform pan. Pour half the batter in pan, top with sliced pears. Sprinkle half the topping over pears. Spread remaining batter over pears. Sprinkle with remaining nut topping. Bake at 350° for about 50 minutes. Cool, remove from pan, place on platter. Slice in wedges. Serve warm, topped with sweetened whipped cream or apple butter.

Submitted by Peifferhaus B&B, Camano Island

♥ Pumpkin Coffee Cake ♥

3 cups flour
2 teaspoons baking
  powder
2 teaspoons baking soda
1 tablespoon cinnamon
1 teaspoon salt
1/2 teaspoon cloves

1/4 teaspoon nutmeg
1/4 teaspoon allspice
1 (16-ounce) can pumpkin
2 cups sugar
1 1/4 cups salad oil
4 eggs
1 cup chopped nuts

Preheat oven to 350°. Grease and flour sides & bottom of springform pan. Sift together flour, baking powder, baking soda, cinnamon, salt, cloves, nutmeg, and allspice. Beat together pumpkin, sugar, salad oil, and eggs, one at a time. Add flour mixture to liquid mixture. Add chopped nuts. Pour into pan. Bake for 40 minutes. Test. Let cool in pan for 10 minutes. Serve with whipped cream or softened and sweetened cream cheese. Makes 12 servings.

Submitted by The Duffy House B&B, Friday Harbor

♥ Raspberry Cream Cheese Coffee Cake ♥

10-6-03 Mike didn't like

2 1/4 cups flour
3/4 cup sugar
3/4 cup margarine or
  butter
1/2 teaspoon baking
  powder
1/2 teaspoon baking soda
1/4 teaspoon salt
3/4 cup dairy sour cream

1 egg
1 teaspoon almond extract   or 1/2 vanilla
8 ounces cream cheese,
  softened
1/4 cup sugar
1 egg
1/2 cup raspberry   } + 1 cup fresh berries
  preserves or sauce
1/2 cup sliced almonds coconut

Preheat oven to 350°. Grease and flour sides and bottom of springform pan. Lightly spoon flour into measuring cup, level off. In large bowl combine flour and 3/4 cup sugar. Using pastry blender, cut in margarine until mixture resembles coarse crumbs. Reserve 1 cup crumb mixture. To remaining mixture, add baking powder, baking soda, salt, sour cream, 1 egg, and almond extract; blend well. Spread batter over bottom and 2" up sides of pan. Batter should be 1/4" thick on sides. In small bowl mix cream cheese, 1/4 cup sugar, and 1 egg; blend well. Pour over batter in pan. Carefully spoon preserves or sauce evenly over cream cheese filling. In small bowl combine 1 cup reserved crumbs and sliced almonds. Sprinkle over top. Bake for 45 to 55 minutes or until filling is set. Cool for 20 minutes. Remove pan sides, cut, and serve. Makes 16 servings.

Store in Fridge

Submitted by The Duffy House B&B, Friday Harbor

♥   # Sour Cream Coffee Cake   ♥

2 cups sifted flour
1 1/2 teaspoons baking powder
1 teaspoon baking soda
1/2 teaspoon salt

1/2 cup butter
1 cup sugar
2 eggs
1 teaspoon vanilla
1 cup sour cream

Nut Mix:
1/2 cup sugar
2 teaspoons cinnamon

1/2 cup coconut
1/2 cup chopped walnuts

Combine nut mix ingredients and set aside. Sift together flour, baking powder, baking soda and salt. Cream butter and 1 cup sugar. Beat until fluffy. Beat in eggs, one at a time. Blend in vanilla. Add sifted dry ingredients alternately with sour cream. Put 1/3 of batter into greased loaf pan. Top with half the nut mix. Add another 1/3 of batter, the other half of the nut mix, and the final 1/3 of batter. Bake at 350° for 45 to 55 minutes.

Submitted by Spink's Ocean View, Whidbey Island - Clinton

Helpful Hints for Yeast Breads:

- *Rinse your mixing bowl in hot water before beginning your bread making.*
- *Sprinkle bread board or countertop very lightly with flour. Spoon dough onto surface and let it sit for 10 minutes before kneading. This wait will enable the dough to become firmer and be less sticky, and therefore easier to knead.*
- *Keep rising dough away from drafts and at a temperature of 85°. If too warm, bread will be dark, coarse, and taste "yeasty." If too cool, bread will be heavy and solid.*
- *Loaves or rolls are ready to be baked when they retain the impression after being lightly touched. Glass, darkened metal, or dull-finished aluminum pans are ideal for baking bread. (They absorb heat and give bread a good brown crust.)*
- *Bread is done when loaves shrink from the pan and sound hollow when top crust is tapped with finger.*
- *Loaves should be removed from pans immediately and placed on cooling racks. It is not necessary to cover the bread when it is cooling; doing so will make it turn soggy.*

♥ ## Strawberry Rhubarb Coffee Cake ♥

Filling:
3 cups sliced fresh or
frozen rhubarb
1 quart fresh straw-
berries, mashed
2 tablespoons lemon juice
1 cup sugar
1/3 cup cornstarch

Topping:
1/4 cup butter, melted
3/4 cup flour
3/4 cup sugar

Cake:
3 cups flour
1 cup sugar
1 teaspoon baking
powder
1 teaspoon baking soda
1/2 teaspoon salt
1 cup butter or margarine,
cut into pieces
1 1/2 cups buttermilk
2 eggs
1 teaspoon vanilla

For Filling: In large saucepan combine rhubarb, strawberries, and lemon juice. Cover and cook over medium heat about 5 minutes. Combine sugar and cornstarch; stir into saucepan. Bring to a boil, stirring constantly until thickened; remove from heat and set aside. For Cake: In large bowl combine flour, sugar, baking powder, baking soda, and salt. Cut in butter until mixture resembles coarse crumbs. Beat buttermilk, eggs, and vanilla; stir into crumb mixture. Spread half of batter evenly into greased baking dish. Carefully spread filling on top. Drop remaining batter by tablespoonfuls over filling. For Topping: Melt butter in saucepan over low heat. Remove from heat; stir in flour and sugar until mixture resembles coarse crumbs. Sprinkle over batter. Lay foil on lower rack to catch any spillovers. Place coffee cake on middle rack; bake at 350° for 40 to 45 minutes. Cool in dish; cut into squares. Makes 16 servings.

Submitted by The Duffy House B&B, Friday Harbor

♥ Wild Blackberry Coffee Cake ♥

Cake:
2 1/2 cups sifted
  flour
1/2 cup sugar
1/4 teaspoon salt
2 teaspoons baking
  powder
1/4 teaspoon nutmeg
1/4 cup melted butter or
  margarine
1 large egg
1 cup milk
1/2 teaspoon almond
  flavoring

1/3 cup coconut
2 cups blackberries, fresh
  or frozen

Topping:
1/3 cup brown sugar
1/3 cup walnuts,
  chopped

Glaze:
1/2 cup confectioners
  sugar
2 teaspoons light cream
  or milk

Preheat oven to 375°. Grease 9" fluted pastry pan; set aside. Combine all dry ingredients in bowl. Add melted butter, egg, milk, and almond flavoring; beat until smooth. Spread 2/3 of mixture on bottom of pastry pan. Top with coconut. Scatter 1 cup blackberries over coconut and push berries slightly into batter. Pour remaining batter on top, in the center, and smooth toward edges. It will not cover entire cake. Scatter remaining berries. Top with brown sugar and nuts. Bake for 40 to 45 minutes or until cake tests done with toothpick. Frozen berries will cause cake to bake slower. Cool. Mix glaze ingredients and drizzle over top in a spiral swirl starting from the center and working out. Garnish with blackberry leaves. Makes 8 servings.

Submitted by Eagles Nest Inn, Whidbey Island - Langley

Pancakes ~ Waffles

Melissa Pigg ©

Napkin Folding

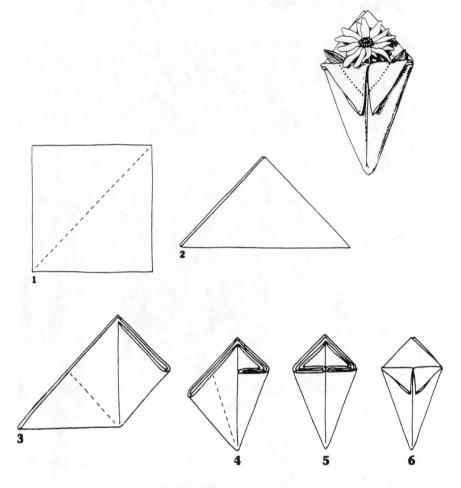

Flower Basket

1. Fold the napkin in half to form a triangle.
2. Place with the fold along the bottom edge.
3. Bring the right and left points up to the center as shown.
4. Then fold right edge to the center.
5. Fold the left edge to the center.
6. Fold down the corner points of the top layer.

♥ # Blueberry/Huckleberry Pancakes
With Berry Sauce ♥

2 cups buttermilk
2 eggs
1 teaspoon salt
1 teaspoon baking
  soda

1/4 cup oil
2 tablespoons sugar
1 1/2 - 1 3/4 cups flour
1 cup frozen blueberries
  or huckleberries

Berry Sauce:
2 cups blueberries or
  huckleberries
2 tablespoons lemon juice

1/3 cup sugar, or to taste
2 teaspoons cornstarch
2 tablespoons water

Combine buttermilk, eggs, salt, baking soda, oil and 2 tablespoons sugar and whisk. Add flour a little at a time, whisking well. Stir 1 tablespoon flour into berries. Keep berries frozen and add to batter as needed. If berries sit too long in batter pancakes will be blue! Cook on griddle in oil, not butter. For Berry Sauce: Place berries in saucepan with lemon juice and sugar. Cook gently until bubbly. Do not overcook. Mix cornstarch with water until smooth. Add a little at a time to berries until desired consistency. Serve with these pancakes, waffles or French toast. Offer small bowls of lemon curd and Devonshire cream as accompaniment.

Submitted by The Fotheringham House, Spokane

www.wbbg.com

♥ **Blue Corn Pancakes** ♥
With Sweet Pineapple Salsa

1 cup blue cornmeal
2 tablespoons sugar
1/2 teaspoon salt
1 cup boiling water
1 egg
3/4 cup milk

2 tablespoons melted
  butter
1/2 cup flour
2 teaspoons baking
  powder

Pineapple Salsa:
1 fresh whole pineapple,
  cut into chunks
1 cup light corn syrup

1 cup dried assorted fruit
Juice and grated rind of
  1 large lime

Preheat griddle or large fry pan. Combine cornmeal, sugar, salt and boiling water in large mixing bowl, let stand for 10 minutes. In separate bowl beat egg, milk and melted butter and add to cornmeal mixture. Sift flour and baking powder and add to batter and mix well. On preheated grill or pan, use about 1/4 cup for each pancake. Turn when top of pancake is bubbly. For Salsa: Cut fresh pineapple into small chunks. Place in a bowl along with any juice. Add corn syrup, dried fruit, lime juice and grated rind. Mix well and set aside to let the dried fruit absorb the flavors. We serve the salsa on the side to allow our guests to top their pancakes. Makes about 12 pancakes.

Submitted by Channel House, Anacortes

♥ **Cottage Cheese Hotcakes** ♥

3 eggs, separated
3/4 cup cottage cheese
1/4 cup flour
1/4 teaspoon salt

1 1/2 teaspoons cream
  of tartar
Sour cream
Jam

Do not prepare batter ahead. Beat egg yolks until thick. Add cottage cheese and beat well. Stir in flour and salt. Beat egg whites and cream of tartar until stiff. Fold into batter. Bake on 380° griddle. Make each hotcake about 3" in diameter. Hotcake is done when sides are dry to light touch with finger. Serve immediately with one teaspoon each sour cream and jam on each hotcake. Makes 3 servings.

Submitted by The Log Castle B&B, Whidbey Island - Langley

♥ Gingerbread Pancakes With Lemon Sauce ♥

1 1/3 cups complete
  pancake mix
1/2 teaspoon ginger

1 teaspoon cinnamon
1/4 cup molasses
1 1/4 cups water

Lemon Sauce:
1/2 cup sugar
1 tablespoon cornstarch
Pinch of nutmeg
1 cup hot water

2 tablespoons margarine
1/2 teaspoon grated
  lemon rind
2 tablespoons lemon
  juice

Stir together pancake mix, ginger and cinnamon. Add molasses and water to the pancake mixture. Stir until combined. Batter may be lumpy. Grease seasoned pancake griddle, if necessary, and place over medium heat until a few drops of water dance on the hot griddle. Cook pancakes on first side until they are puffed, full of bubbles and look dry at edges. Then turn and cook until second side is browned. Serve with hot Lemon Sauce: In medium saucepan mix sugar, cornstarch and nutmeg. Gradually mix in hot water. Cook, stirring, over medium heat until mixture is thick and clear. Add margarine, lemon rind and lemon juice, stirring until margarine melts. Serve hot. Makes 3 - 4 servings.

Submitted by Miller Tree Inn, Forks

♥ Grandma's Oatmeal Buttermilk Hotcakes ♥

1 1/2 cups quick cooking
  oatmeal
2 cups good quality
  buttermilk
2 extra large eggs,
  separated

1/2 cup all purpose flour
1 teaspoon baking powder
1 teaspoon baking soda
1 teaspoon sugar or
  substitute (opt.)
1/2 teaspoon salt

Soak oatmeal in buttermilk for 20 minutes. Separate eggs and put yolks into buttermilk mixture. Sift dry ingredients into buttermilk mixture and stir just until blended. Beat egg whites until peaks form, then fold into batter. Cook on hot griddle until golden on both sides. Eat and enjoy! Recipe may be doubled.

Submitted by Old Tjomsland House, Vashon Island

♥ Illahee Manor Baked Pancakes ♥

1/2 cup butter	1 teaspoon cinnamon
5 eggs	1 tablespoon vanilla
2 cups milk	1 cup cottage cheese
1 cup flour	1 teaspoon baking
1/3 cup sugar	powder

Preheat oven to 400°. Cut butter into small pieces and place into 6 individual ramekins. Heat in oven until butter is browned. Combine remaining ingredients in blender until frothy (for about 1 minute). Pour blended mixture into hot dishes and bake for 40 minutes. Pancake will rise and brown. Remove from oven and serve. Pancake will fall in about 5 minutes. Serve with powdered sugar and berries.

Submitted by Illahee Manor B&B, Bremerton

♥ Lavender Buttermilk Pancakes ♥

3 cups flour	3/4 cup milk
2 tablespoons sugar	3 large eggs
1 1/2 teaspoons salt	1 teaspoon vanilla
1 1/2 teaspoons baking powder	6 tablespoons butter, melted
1/2 teaspoon baking soda	2 tablespoons lavender buds, chopped
2 1/4 cups buttermilk	

Mix flour, sugar, salt, baking powder, and baking soda. Warm buttermilk and milk to room temperature. Beat eggs until frothy. Combine eggs, warmed milk, vanilla, melted butter, and lavender. Combine wet and dry ingredients. Do not overmix - small lumps should remain. Cook on lightly greased griddle. Will hold in 200° oven if covered with towel, for 15+ minutes.

Submitted by WindSong Inn, Orcas Island, San Juan Islands

♥ Magic Strawberry Pancake Basket ♥

Strawberry Cream Filling:
3 pints strawberries,
  stems removed & halved
1/2 cup sugar (granulated
  or powdered)

Sour Cream Topping:
2 cups (1 pint) sour
  cream
1/4 cup brown sugar

Pancake Basket:
2 eggs
1/2 cup milk
1/4 teaspoon salt, or
  to taste

1/2 cup flour
1 tablespoon butter or
  margarine

One to two hours before serving: Prepare Strawberry Cream Filling by stirring together strawberries and sugar, and set aside. Mix sour cream and brown sugar together for topping. Refrigerate until ready to use. To make Pancake Basket: Place oven rack in center of oven and preheat to 450°. In small bowl mix eggs, milk, salt and flour. Put butter in pie or quiche dish, place in oven for 2 minutes or until butter is melted. Swirl to coat bottom and immediately pour in egg batter. Bake for 15 minutes, reduce oven temperature to 350° and bake for 8 to 10 minutes, or until puffed and golden brown. Remove from oven, lift out basket and place on serving plate. Spoon strawberries in the center and top with sour cream. To serve, cut in wedges. Makes 4 - 6 servings.

Submitted by Trumpeter Inn B&B, San Juan Island

♥ Marlene's Cottage Cheese Pancakes ♥

4 eggs, separated
1/4 cup all purpose flour
1/4 cup small curd
  cottage cheese

1/4 cup dairy sour
  cream
Dash of salt

In medium bowl beat egg yolks, flour, cottage cheese, and sour cream until blended. In small bowl beat egg whites with a dash of salt until stiff. Gently fold egg whites into egg yolk mixture. Spoon onto moderately hot, greased griddle, spreading each pancake to about a 4" diameter. When underside is brown, turn pancake over, flatten slightly with spatula and cook until golden. To increase recipe: 6 eggs, 1/2 cup flour, 1/2 cup cottage cheese, 1/2 cup sour cream OR 8 eggs, 1 cup flour, 1 cup cottage cheese, 1 cup sour cream.

Submitted by Old Tjomsland House, Vashon Island

♥ ## Millie's Wild Huckleberry Pancakes ♥

1 cup sifted flour
1 teaspoon baking powder
1/4 teaspoon salt
1 tablespoon sugar
1/2 teaspoon baking soda
1 cup sour cream

2 eggs
3 tablespoons melted
  butter
1/3 cup sweet milk
2/3 cup wild
  huckleberries

Sift flour, baking powder, salt, sugar, and baking soda together. Beat sour cream, eggs, and melted butter together. Add to dry ingredients. Stir, adding enough milk to get desired thickness. Do not beat! A few small lumps are fine. Fold in wild huckleberries. Cook until golden. Makes approximately 6 pancakes.

Submitted by The Farm - a B&B, Trout Lake

♥ ## Oven Puff Pancake ♥

1/4 cup butter or
  margarine
3 ounces cream cheese
3/4 cup flour

<u>Optional side topping:</u>
1 cup sour cream

3 eggs
3/4 cup milk
Sliced fruit & powdered
  sugar

3 tablespoons brown
  sugar

Place butter or margarine in shallow 2 or 3 quart baking dish or in 9" pie or cake pan. Place container in 425° oven until butter melts, approximately 5 minutes. Meanwhile put cream cheese, flour, eggs, and milk into blender or food processor and blend until smooth. Remove pan from oven and pour batter into melted butter. Return to oven and bake for 25 to 30 minutes or until pancake is puffed and brown. To serve, fill with sliced fruit (strawberries, peaches, mangos, kiwi, blackberries, etc.) and sprinkle with powdered sugar. If desired, mix topping together and offer on the side. Makes 4 servings.

Submitted by Heaven's Edge B&B, Silverdale

♥ ## Panukakku - Finnish Pancake ♥

3 eggs, beaten	3 teaspoons sugar
1 cup milk	1/4 teaspoon salt
1/2 cup flour	1 tablespoon butter

Preheat oven to 375°. Put pie pan in oven to heat. Beat eggs, add milk, and beat again. Add flour, sugar, and salt. Beat again, but do not overbeat. Remove pie pan; place butter in bottom and pour batter into dish. Bake for 15 to 20 minutes in center of oven. When done, top with butter, sugar and cinnamon, or jam.

Submitted by Scandinavian Gardens Inn, Long Beach Peninsula

___

♥ ## Peach Melba Dutch Babies ♥

6 tablespoons margarine	2 tablespoons sugar
2 peaches, peeled & sliced	1 teaspoon vanilla
	1/2 teaspoon salt
6 eggs	1/2 teaspoon cinnamon
1 1/2 cups milk	1 cup raspberry puree
1 cup flour	Fresh raspberries/garnish

Preheat oven to 425°. Melt margarine in 9" x 13" baking dish (or four individual au gratin dishes). Set peaches aside. Whirl eggs, milk, flour, sugar, vanilla, salt, and cinnamon in blender until well mixed. Pour batter into baking dish or dishes and bake until puffed and golden, about 20 to 25 minutes. Remove from oven and quickly place peach slices on top. Drizzle with raspberry puree and serve immediately. Garnish with fresh raspberries.

Submitted by Commencement Bay B&B, Tacoma

♥   Peach Upside Down Pancake   ♥

Butter
3 tablespoons brown
  sugar
2 teaspoons cinnamon
4 peaches, peeled &
  halved

1 cup pancake mix,
  prepared according to
  directions on package
Whipped cream, slivered
  almonds, maraschino
  cherry bits, for garnish

Generously butter a round 9" pie plate. Sprinkle the bottom of the pan with brown sugar and cinnamon. Place peaches in pan, with the cut side up. Pour prepared pancake mix over peaches. Bake at 400° for 30 to 35 minutes. Cool in pan for 5 minutes before inverting onto plate. Before you take it to the table, fancy it up with a generous design of whipped cream, slivered almonds and maraschino cherry bits. You can substitute peeled apples. Makes a generous portion shared between two people and looks magnificent. Excellent dish for the vegetarian guest or those who are not allowed egg in their diet.

Submitted by Maple Meadow B&B, Point Roberts

♥   Potato Pancakes   ♥

4 large potatoes, grated
2 egg yolks
1/2 cup flour
1 teaspoon salt

1/2 teaspoon baking
  powder
2 egg whites,
  beaten

Mix ingredients in order given. Fry on hot griddle until golden brown.

Submitted by 1908 Cooney Mansion, Aberdeen (Cosmopolis)

♥ **Stoltz House Secret Pancakes** ♥

1 quart lowfat
   buttermilk
2 tablespoons granulated
   sugar
1 pkg. active dry yeast
1 teaspoon salt
4 cups flour

2 tablespoons baking
   soda
2 tablespoons baking
   powder
1/4 cup canola oil
10 eggs
1 cup heavy cream

Combine buttermilk, granulated sugar and yeast. Stir in a mixture of salt, flour, baking soda and baking powder. Stir all to mix well. Stir in the oil. Beat the eggs using an electric mixer for about 5 minutes or until light yellow and thickened; carefully fold into the buttermilk/flour mixture. Cover and refrigerate overnight. The next morning stir in heavy cream. Cook on hot griddle. Bonus: The pancake batter will keep for a week in the refrigerator. The batter may darken, but this is from the yeast. Just stir lightly before cooking. This recipe will feed an army! Top with huckleberry sauce and whipped cream flavored with almond extract. Absolutely delicious!

Submitted by Marianna Stoltz House B&B, Spokane

♥ **Swedish Pancakes With Huckleberry Sauce** ♥

Pancake:
2 eggs
1 cup milk
1 cup flour
1/2 teaspoon salt
1 tablespoon sugar
1/4 cup melted butter

Sauce:
1/3 cup sugar
1 tablespoon cornstarch
2 cups huckleberries
2 tablespoons lemon
   juice
1/3 cup water

Combine eggs, and milk; add remaining ingredients. Bake in buttered iron skillet using enough batter to cover thinly. Brown on each side, roll, and keep warm until all are cooked. For Sauce: Combine ingredients in saucepan; cook over medium heat until thickened. Serve warm or cool. Great on ice cream and cheesecake too!

Submitted by Waverly Place B&B, Spokane

♥   # World's Best Buttermilk Pancakes

1 cup buttermilk
1 egg, room temperature
3 tablespoons butter,
    melted

3/4 cup all purpose flour
1/2 teaspoon salt
1 teaspoon baking
    soda

Combine buttermilk, egg and melted butter briskly in mixing bowl, until the mixture is well mixed and smooth. Stir flour, salt and baking soda in a small bowl so they are blended. Stir into the buttermilk mixture only until the dry ingredients are moistened - leaving the batter lumpy. Heat your griddle to medium hot. Spray with Pam® and measure out about 1/3 cup of batter for each pancake. Cook until a few bubbles break on top. Turn the pancake over and cook briefly. Keep pancakes warm in oven until enough are cooked to serve. Makes about 7 (4" - 5") pancakes.

Submitted by The Green Cape Cod B&B, Tacoma

♥   # Apple Stuffed Crepes   ♥

Crepes:
3 eggs
1 1/4 cups milk
3/4 cup sifted all purpose
    flour
1 tablespoon sugar
1/2 teaspoon salt

Filling:
2 tablespoons butter
1 cup sugar
1 tablespoon cinnamon
6 apples, peeled &
    sliced
Powdered sugar/garnish

For Crepes: Beat eggs. Stir in milk. Sift dry ingredients; add to egg mixture, mixing until smooth. Grease frying pan. Pour 3/4 of a ladle into hot frying pan. Cook both sides and set aside. For Filling: Peel and slice apples. Melt butter in sauté pan. Add sugar, cinnamon and apples. Cook until apples become tender. Fill crepes with apples and top with powdered sugar. Makes about 12 crepes.

Submitted by The White Rose Inn, Enumclaw

♥ **Breakfast Crepes** ♥

24 pork sausage links
12 eggs
Garlic salt & fresh
  pepper, to taste

1 cup mixed Swiss &
  cheddar cheese, grated

Crepes:
3 cups whole or canned
  milk, warmed
4 tablespoons melted
  butter

6 eggs
4 tablespoons sugar
Pinch of salt
2 1/2 cups flour

Brown and fully cook sausage links. Scramble 12 eggs and season with garlic salt and fresh pepper. Add grated cheese to scrambled eggs; set aside. For Crepes: Warm milk and add melted butter. Beat and stir in eggs. Mix in sugar and salt, beat well. Blend in flour and mix all ingredients well. Using an electric Teflon® crepe maker, make crepes. Fill each crepe with a cooked sausage and some cooked eggs. Roll up and place on buttered baking sheet. Warm in oven at 300° for 25 minutes or so. Serve warm topped with pure maple syrup or warm apricot jam. These may be made ahead of time, refrigerated or frozen. Makes 8 - 10 servings.

Submitted by Peifferhaus B&B, Camano Island

Hints On Cooking Crepes:

- *Heat your crepe pan on medium heat. Brush the bottom of the pan with melted butter.*
- *Pour 1/4 cup of batter into the pan. Swirl the batter to coat bottom of the pan. Quickly pour any excess back into your mixing bowl. (You should be left with a very thin layer of batter.)*
- *Seconds later, when underside is golden, lift up an edge with a spatula. Pick crepe up with your fingers. Flip over to cook other side (2 - 3 seconds).*
- *When done, remove quickly. Place on plate or wax paper. Serve when ready. Crepes will also freeze well.*

♥ Buttermilk Crepes ♥

Crepes:
2 eggs
1 cup buttermilk
2 tablespoons melted
  butter

1/3 cup water
1 cup sifted flour
1/2 teaspoon salt
1/4 teaspoon pumpkin
  pie spice

Crepe Filling:
3 ounces softened
  cream cheese
1/3 cup sour cream

1/3 cup yogurt
1/2 teaspoon vanilla

Citrus Syrup:
1 cup sugar
1 cup butter

6 ounces orange juice
  concentrate
1 teaspoon vanilla

For Crepes: Place wet ingredients in blender in the order given. Cover and blend at high speed for 20 to 30 seconds. Then add all dry ingredients. Cover and blend at high speed, stopping to scrape down the sides of the container. Blend a few more seconds until smooth. Cook according to crepe directions. Makes about 14 - 16 crepes. For Filling: Blend all ingredients together with an electric mixer until smooth and creamy. To assemble crepes: Spread 2 tablespoons filling on each warm crepe. Fold or roll, whichever is preferred. Place in a row on serving plate. Cover crepes with fresh fruit of choice.   Peaches, blackberries, blueberries, huckleberries or strawberries are best. Drizzle warm citrus syrup over the top of fruit. For Syrup: Combine all ingredients, except vanilla, in saucepan. Cook on low heat until sugar is completely dissolved. DO NOT BOIL. Add vanilla. Cool for 10 minutes, then whip at high speed with electric mixer for 3 minutes. This will make it very silky and keep it from separating. Store in tight-fitting jar in refrigerator. It will keep for a month You can heat it prior to serving. Try it on crepes, waffles, French toast, on ice cream or stirred into yogurt. Dust Buttermilk Crepes with powdered sugar and serve.

Submitted by Edenwild Inn, Lopez Island

♥ **Buttermilk Waffles** ♥

2 cups flour
2 teaspoons baking
  powder
1 teaspoon baking soda

1/2 teaspoon salt
2 cups buttermilk
3 large eggs, beaten
1/4 cup melted butter

Heat waffle iron. In large bowl combine flour, baking powder, baking soda, and salt. Stir buttermilk into dry ingredients. Add beaten eggs, and butter. Ladle onto waffle iron to cover 2/3 of grid. Bake about 5 minutes. Keep warm in slow oven with door slightly ajar.

Submitted by Tudor Inn, Port Angeles

♥ **Cornmeal Yeast Waffles** ♥

2 cups milk
1/2 cup warm water
  (105° - 115°)
1 pkg. active dry yeast
1/3 cup butter, melted
1 teaspoon salt

1 tablespoon sugar
2 cups flour
1 cup yellow cornmeal
2 eggs, slightly beaten
1/2 teaspoon baking
  soda

Scald milk, and cool to lukewarm. Put warm water in large bowl. Sprinkle in yeast and stir to dissolve. Add milk, butter, salt, sugar, flour, and cornmeal. Mix until batter is smooth. Cover and let stand at room temperature overnight. When ready to bake, add eggs, and baking soda. Beat well. Bake in pre-heated waffle iron. Makes 3 servings.

Submitted by Kangaroo House B&B on Orcas Island,
Eastsound / Orcas Island

♥ Grandma's Country Waffles ♥

2 cups sifted flour
2 tablespoons sugar
3 teaspoons baking
  powder

1/2 teaspoon salt
3 eggs, separated
2 cups milk
1/2 cup melted shortening

Sift flour, sugar, baking powder, and salt together into mixing bowl. Separate eggs; combine egg yolks and milk. Blend liquid with dry ingredients. Stir in melted shortening. Beat egg whites until stiff and fold into batter. Bake on hot waffle iron. Top with favorite topping.

Submitted by The Shepherd's Inn B&B, Salkum

♥ Orange Waffles ♥

4 eggs, separated
3 cups flour
4 teaspoons baking
  powder
1/4 teaspoon salt
1/2 cup sugar

2 cups milk (or more)
2/3 stick butter,
  softened
Grated rind from 1
  orange
1 teaspoon vanilla

Beat egg whites until stiff. In separate bowl sift flour and baking powder. Add salt and sugar; mix. Add egg yolks, milk, and softened butter. Mix. Add orange rind and vanilla. Gently fold into egg whites. Bake in hot greased waffle iron.

Submitted by Inn at Barnum Point, Camano Island

♥   # Pumpkin Waffles   ♥

1 cup pumpkin, cooked
1 1/2 cups milk
3 eggs
2 tablespoons butter,
  melted
1 cup all purpose flour
1/3 cup whole wheat
  flour

2 teaspoons baking
  powder
1/2 teaspoon salt
2 tablespoons sugar
1/8 teaspoon ground
  nutmeg
1/8 teaspoon pumpkin
  pie spice

In large bowl stir together pumpkin, milk, eggs and butter. In separate bowl sift together flours, baking powder, salt, sugar, nutmeg and pumpkin pie spice. Add sifted ingredients to pumpkin mixture, stirring thoroughly until combined. Preheat waffle iron (Belgian waffle iron is preferred), spoon in batter and bake until golden. Top with maple syrup, whipped cream flavored with a dash of ginger and freshly grated nutmeg.

Submitted by Skagit Bay Hideaway, La Conner

Hints About Waffle Making:

- *A properly seasoned waffle iron will not need grease or pan spray. Brush away any crumbs from the last use.*
- *Heat up your waffle iron until the heat indicator shows that it is ready.*
- *Pour enough batter to fill approximately two-thirds of the waffle iron.*

♥ ## Stoltz House Waffles ♥

1 pkg. dry yeast
1 teaspoon sugar
2 1/2 cups warm water
 (105° - 115°)
3 cups all purpose
 flour
1/2 teaspoon salt

1/2 teaspoon baking
 powder
2/3 cup instant nonfat
 dry milk powder
1/3 cup vegetable oil
2 large eggs

Dissolve yeast and sugar in warm water in large mixing bowl. Let stand 5 minutes. Add flour and next five ingredients. Beat at medium speed of electric mixer until blended. Cover and chill 8 hours. Bake in preheated, oiled waffle iron. Serve with Mandarin Strawberry Topping (see recipe on page 27). Makes 20 - 4" waffles.

Submitted by Marianna Stoltz House B&B, Spokane

To Add Protein To Your Breakfast Dishes:

If you wish to increase the protein quality of your breads, pancakes, waffles, or pastries, add any of the following ingredients:

Almonds
Bran flakes
Buttermilk
Cashew butter
Eggs, egg whites
Garbanzo bean flour
Milk, dry milk
Peanut butter

Protein powder
Pumpkin seeds
Quinoa
Soy milk
Sunflower seeds
Walnuts
All other seeds & nuts
Yogurt

French Toast

Napkin Folding

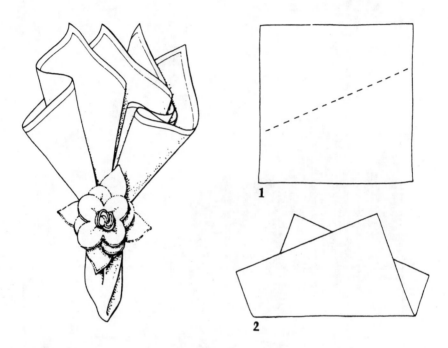

1

2

Bouquet

1. Fold the napkin in half diagonally as shown.
2. Place the folded edge at the bottom. Hold the napkin in the center of this edge and pull it through a napkin ring.

♥ Apricot Cheese Almond Stuffed French Toast ♥

3 slices French bread, cut diagonally	3 tablespoons cream cheese
2 eggs	1 tablespoon apricot jam
Dash of cinnamon	
Dash of nutmeg	1 drop almond extract
1 tablespoon custard powder	1 teaspoon chopped almonds
3/4 cup milk	Powdered sugar (opt.)

Whisk eggs, cinnamon, nutmeg, custard powder, and milk together with wire whip. Stir together cream cheese, jam, almond extract, and chopped almonds for stuffing; set aside. Dip bread slices into whisked eggs. Fry on griddle until golden brown. Prepare like a sandwich, placing stuffing ingredients between 2 slices of bread, and keeping in warm oven. Serve with warm apricot syrup. Optional: Sift a light sprinkle of powdered sugar over French toast and sprinkle with a few sliced almonds.

Submitted by The Fountains B&B, Gig Harbor

♥ Baked Apple French Toast ♥

1/2 cup butter	2 tablespoons vanilla
1/2 cup brown sugar	6 - 10 slices bread (white, wheat, sour-dough or French)
4 large green apples, peeled & sliced	
8 eggs	1 tablespoon cinnamon
3 1/2 cups milk	

Melt butter; add brown sugar and apples and simmer 1 to 2 minutes. Pour into 9" x 13" pan and let cool. Beat together eggs, milk, and vanilla. Slice bread in half and layer over apples to cover whole dish. Pour egg mixture over all making sure all bread is wet. Sprinkle with cinnamon. Bake at 350° until golden brown and puffy for 40 to 50 minutes. Cut into squares and serve with powdered sugar or favorite syrup.

Submitted by Waverly Place B&B, Spokane

♥ Baked Blueberry French Toast ♥

8 ounces light cream
cheese, softened
1/3 cup maple syrup
1/2 cup light sour cream
1/2 cup plain lowfat
yogurt
2/3 cup lowfat milk
8 eggs
1/2 teaspoon cinnamon

3/4 teaspoon nutmeg
1 teaspoon vanilla
8 large slices French
bread
1 1/2 cups frozen
blueberries
Cooking spray
Maple syrup for
serving

Combine cream cheese, 1/3 cup maple syrup, sour cream, yogurt and milk until smooth. Add eggs, spices and vanilla. Beat together with cream cheese mixture. Spray a 9" x 13" baking dish with cooking spray. Lay 4 slices of bread in pan. Sprinkle with half of the blueberries. Pour on half of the cream cheese mixture. Layer on the remaining bread; sprinkle on remaining berries and pour cream cheese mixture over all. Cover and refrigerate overnight. Remove 30 minutes before baking. Bake covered with foil at 350° for 30 minutes. Uncover and continue baking for 30 minutes more. Serve with maple syrup. Makes 6 - 8 servings. From *Beyond the Moon Cookbook* by Ginny Callan.

Submitted by Soundview B&B, Seattle

♥ Baked French Toast ♥

1 loaf thin sliced
French bread
8 ounces light
cream cheese
8 - 12 eggs
1/2 cup maple syrup

1 cup milk (can use
1/2 cup more milk,
if desired)
1 teaspoon vanilla
1 teaspoon cinnamon
2 tablespoons sugar

Grease an 11" x 13" baking dish. Cut bread into large cubes and line bottom of dish with 1/3 of bread cubes. Dot bread cubes with half (4 ounces) cream cheese. Repeat layers with 1/3 bread cubes and remaining cream cheese. Top layer should be the remaining 1/3 bread cubes. Beat eggs, syrup, milk, vanilla, cinnamon and sugar and pour over all layers to saturate. (Mix up more egg mixture, if needed, to cover bread.) Cover and refrigerate overnight. Bake uncovered at 350° for approximately 40 minutes. Drizzle 1 - 2 cups fruit or berry sauce and additional fresh fruit or berries, if available, over top of baked layers. Sprinkle with powdered sugar. May serve with warm maple syrup on the side. Makes 8 servings.

Submitted by Bosch Gärten B&B, Leavenworth

♥ # Baked Tomato French Toast ♥

Nonstick spray
8 slices toasted whole
wheat bread
8 slices (6 ounces)
Canadian bacon
5 ounces (1 1/4 cups)
grated lowfat sharp
cheddar cheese,
divided

1 cup liquid egg
substitute
1 (12-ounce) can
evaporated skim milk
1/4 teaspoon freshly
grated black pepper
1 pound (5) plum
tomatoes, cored &
thinly sliced

Preheat oven to 350°. Spray 9" x 13" x 2" pan with nonstick spray. Place toasted bread slices in dish and spray. Arrange bacon slices on top and sprinkle with 3/4 cup cheese. Combine egg substitute, milk and pepper. Mix and pour over ingredients in pan. Bake uncovered for 15 minutes or until nearly firm. Remove from oven and arrange tomato slices over the top. Return to oven uncovered for 5 minutes. Remove from oven and sprinkle with 1/2 cup cheese. Makes 6 servings.

Submitted by Hummingbird Inn, Roslyn

www.wbbg.com

♥ ## Blueberry French Toast ♥

12 slices day-old white bread, crusts removed
2 - 8 ounce pkgs. cream cheese
1 cup fresh or frozen blueberries
12 eggs
2 cups milk
1/3 cup maple syrup or honey

Sauce:
1 cup sugar
2 tablespoons cornstarch
1 cup water
1 cup fresh or frozen blueberries
1 tablespoon butter or margarine

Cut bread into 1" cubes; place half in greased 9" x 13" x 2" baking dish. Cut cream cheese into 1" cubes; place over bread. Top with 1 cup blueberries and remaining bread. In large bowl beat eggs. Add milk and syrup; mix well. Pour over bread mixture. Cover and chill 8 hours or overnight. Remove from refrigerator 30 minutes before baking. Cover and bake at 350° for 30 minutes. Uncover; bake 25 to 30 minutes until golden brown and center is set. For Sauce: In saucepan, combine sugar and cornstarch; add water. Bring to a boil over medium heat. Boil for 3 minutes, stirring constantly. Stir in 1 cup blueberries, reduce heat. Simmer for 8 to 10 minutes until berries have burst. Stir in butter until melted; makes 1 3/4 cups sauce. Serve over French Toast. Makes 6 - 8 servings.

Submitted by The Churchyard Inn, Uniontown

www.wbbg.com

♥ ## Brie & Apple Stuffed French Toast ♥

1 long loaf French
bread
1/2 Golden Delicious
apple, sliced
1 medium wedge Brie
cheese
6 eggs

2 cups milk
1/8 teaspoon nutmeg
1/4 teaspoon cinnamon
1 grated whole nutmeg
3 tablespoons freshly
grated orange zest

Slice French bread into 24 - 1/4" slices and place 12 slices in large baking dish. Set other 12 pieces aside. Core apple and thinly slice into 12 pieces. Place 1 apple slice on each piece of French bread in dish. Cut 12 1/8" slices of Brie, removing waxy outer coating and place 1 slice on each apple-topped piece of bread. Place remaining 12 slices bread on top of Brie. In blender mix eggs, milk, nutmeg, and cinnamon well. Pour egg mixture over Brie and apple "sandwiches", turning to ensure even coating on both sides. Allow bread to soak up all of egg mixture. Cook on lightly oiled, covered griddle preheated to 360°. Place "sandwiches" Brie side down, turning once after cheese has begun to melt. Toast should grill to an even golden brown. Serve immediately topped with freshly grated nutmeg and orange zest. Serves well with fresh berries, Canadian bacon, and maple syrup. Serves 4.

Submitted by Chelsea Station on the Park, Seattle

♥ ## Challah French Toast ♥

20 slices challah bread
6 eggs, slightly beaten
2 cups half and half
1/4 cup rum
1 tablespoon orange zest

1 cup sugar
1/2 teaspoon cinnamon
1/2 teaspoon nutmeg
Corn Flakes® cereal
Butter for sautéeing

Crush corn flakes with rolling pin to make crumbs. Set aside. Whisk together eggs, half and half, rum, orange zest, sugar, and spices. Dip challah in egg mixture, then in Corn Flakes® crumbs to coat. Let stand 10 to 15 minutes to absorb before frying in melted butter until crispy and golden brown. Dust with powdered sugar. Serve with maple syrup. Makes 10 servings.

Submitted by Kangaroo House B&B on Orcas Island,
Eastsound / Orcas Island

♥ Cinnamon-Raisin-Orange French Toast ♥

1 loaf of cinnamon-
   raisin bread
Orange juice, to taste

Eggs or egg substitute,
   to taste
Pinch of cinnamon (opt.)

Mix together as much orange juice (substitute for milk in this version), eggs, and cinnamon as needed for the amount of toast you want to prepare. Dip bread in mixture, coating both sides. Fry on hot griddle until lightly browned. This recipe makes a lighter toast, also dairy free, and lowfat. Sprinkle with powdered sugar. No need to use butter or syrup.

Submitted by Hummingbird Inn, Roslyn

♥ Creme Brûlée French Toast ♥

1 stick unsalted butter
1 cup packed brown
   sugar
2 tablespoons light
   corn syrup
1 (8" - 9") loaf French
   bread, cut into 1"
   slices, crust removed

5 large eggs
1 1/2 cups half
   and half
1 teaspoon vanilla
1 teaspoon Grand
   Marnier
1/4 teaspoon salt

In a small heavy saucepan melt butter with brown sugar and corn syrup over moderate heat, stirring, until smooth and pour into a 9" x 12" x 2" baking dish. Cut French bread into 1" slices and remove crust. Arrange bread slices in one layer in baking dish, squeezing them slightly to fit. In a bowl whisk together eggs, half and half, vanilla, Grand Marnier and salt until combined well and pour evenly over bread. Chill bread mixture, covered, for at least 8 hours and up to 1 day. Preheat oven to 350° and bring bread to room temperature. Bake bread mixture, uncovered, in middle of oven until puffed and edges are pale golden, for 35 to 40 minutes.

Submitted by Cascade Mountain Inn, Concrete-Birdsview

♥ ## Decadent Stuffed French Toast ♥

8 ounces cream cheese	1/2 cup milk
1/3 cup sugar	Dash of nutmeg
2 tablespoons lemon juice	Grated orange or lemon peel, to taste
Old-fashioned Italian bread, sliced	1 tablespoon almond or vanilla extract
4 eggs	Berries & powdered sugar

Blend cream cheese, sugar, and lemon juice until creamy. Slice pocket in each slice of bread. Spread cream cheese filling into pocket. Beat eggs, milk, nutmeg, orange or lemon peel, and extract. Dip bread into this mixture and fry on griddle until golden brown. Top with berries and powdered sugar. Makes 4 servings.

Submitted by Argyle House B&B, San Juan Island

Milk Allergies Require Substitutions

If you are cooking for someone who has a milk allergy, there are several substitutions you may use:

Cup per cup options:
- *Almond or other nut milks*
- *Apple juice*
- *Fruit juice (if acidic, add 1 teaspoon of baking soda)*
- *Rice and other grain milks*
- *Soy milk*
- *Water*

♥ **Eggnog French Toast** ♥
With Apple Cider Syrup

Raisin/Cinnamon bread
or croissants, split
lengthwise, as needed

1 1/2 - 2 tablespoons
butter
Eggnog, to taste

Apple Cider Syrup:
1 large Jonagold apple,
chopped, unpeeled
1 tablespoon butter
1 1/2 cups apple cider,
preferably unfiltered
1/4 cup sugar
1/4 cup honey
2 cups sugar

3 tablespoons unsalted
butter, softened
1/4 teaspoon freshly
grated nutmeg
1/8 teaspoon salt
2 tablespoons brandy,
applejack or Calvados
(opt.)

Melt 1 1/2 - 2 tablespoons butter in heavy pan. Dip bread or croissants in eggnog and slow cook until golden on both sides. Serve with Apple Cider Syrup: Chop apple without peeling or coring. Melt 1 tablespoon butter in medium heavy saucepan. Add apple and cook over medium heat, stirring occasionally, until softened, for about 5 minutes. Add apple cider, 1/4 cup sugar and honey. Simmer for about 15 minutes until apples are transparent. Pour through a sieve and, using back of wooden spoon, force the apple through. Return the liquid and the sieved pulp to the saucepan. Add 2 cups sugar, bring to a boil and cook until thick. Remove from the heat and stir in unsalted butter, nutmeg and salt. After butter has melted, liqueur may be added.

Submitted by Glenna's Guthrie Cottage B&B, Sequim

♥Glenna's Guthrie Cottage Orange French Toast♥

2 large egg whites,
lightly beaten
2/3 cup skim milk
1 tablespoon grated
orange rind

1 tablespoon margarine,
divided
8 thin slices wheat
bread

In a shallow bowl or pie pan whisk the egg whites, milk and orange rind. Melt 1/4 of the margarine in a heavy 12" skillet. Preheat oven to 200°. Quickly dip bread slices in the egg mixture; turn to coat both sides. Place in skillet and cook for 3 minutes or until brown on each side. Prepare the remaining bread slices the same way. Keep the cooked slices warm by placing them on a platter in the oven.

Submitted by Glenna's Guthrie Cottage B&B, Sequim

♥   Granny's Apple French Toast   ♥

1 cup brown sugar,
packed
1/2 cup butter (do not
use margarine)
2 tablespoons light
corn syrup
4 Granny Smith apples,
peeled & sliced

3 eggs
1 cup half and half
1 teaspoon vanilla
extract
9 slices day-old French
bread

Sauce:
1 (10-ounce) jar apple
jelly

1/2 teaspoon pumpkin
pie spice
1 cup applesauce

In a small saucepan combine brown sugar, butter and corn syrup; cook over low heat until thick. Pour into an ungreased 9" x 13" pan, arranging apple slices on top of syrup. In a mixing bowl beat eggs, half and half and vanilla. Dip French bread in egg mixture and arrange over top of apple slices. Cover and refrigerate overnight. Remove from refrigerator 30 minutes before baking and uncover. Bake at 350° for 35 to 40 minutes or until the top of the bread is browned. Combine sauce ingredients and cook over medium heat until the jelly is melted and warm. Serve French toast with apple slices up and spoon the warm sauce on top.

Submitted by The Rose of Gig Harbor, a B&B Inn, Gig Harbor

♥ # Krispie French Toast ♥

12 beaten eggs
1 1/2 cups milk
1 teaspoon vanilla
1/2 teaspoon ground
  cinnamon

6 cups crushed Rice
  Krispies® cereal
16 slices hazelnut/
  poppyseed bread
Canola oil for frying

Beat together eggs, milk, vanilla, and cinnamon. Finely crush cereal. Dip bread slices in egg mixture (about 30 seconds on each side), then dip slices in crushed cereal. Cook bread slices in small amount of canola oil on a griddle until each side is golden brown. Serve piping hot with pure maple syrup. Makes 8 servings.

Submitted by Green Gables Inn, Walla Walla

♥ # Orange Crumb French Toast ♥

2 eggs
1/4 teaspoon salt
2/3 cup orange juice
3/4 cup fine dry bread
  crumbs
1 teaspoon grated
  orange peel
8 slices white bread

3 tablespoons shortening
1 cup maple-flavored or
  maple-blended syrup
1/4 cup orange juice
1/4 teaspoon nutmeg
1 teaspoon grated
  orange peel
Butter or margarine

Combine eggs, salt, and 2/3 cup orange juice; beat together thoroughly. Combine bread crumbs with 1 teaspoon grated orange peel. Dip bread slices in orange-egg mixture, then in crumb mixture, turning slices to coat evenly. Brown on both sides in shortening on hot griddle. Meanwhile combine maple syrup with 1/4 cup orange juice, nutmeg, and 1 teaspoon grated orange peel; simmer for 5 minutes. Serve French toast with hot orange syrup and butter. Makes 4 servings.

Submitted by 1908 Cooney Mansion, Aberdeen (Cosmopolis)

♥ # Orange French Toast ♥

1 loaf French bread, sliced 1" thick	1 cup orange juice
1/2 cup margarine, melted	1/4 cup sugar
1/4 cup honey	2 teaspoons grated orange peel
2 teaspoons cinnamon	1/2 teaspoon salt
6 eggs	1/2 teaspoon cinnamon
1 cup milk	3 cups crushed Corn Flakes® cereal

Combine margarine, honey, and cinnamon and pour evenly into 2 - 9" x 13" glass baking pans. Mix eggs, milk, orange juice, sugar, orange peel, salt, and cinnamon. Dip bread slices into egg mixture, then into Corn Flake® crumbs. Coat both sides. Place slices over cinnamon mixture in pans. Pour remaining egg mixture over slices. Bake at 400° for 20 minutes. Turn over once halfway through baking. Serve with sliced apples cooked with brown sugar, margarine, and cinnamon OR Honey Butter: Mix together 1/2 stick margarine, 1/4 teaspoon grated orange, and 1 teaspoon honey.

Submitted by All Seasons River Inn, Leavenworth

www.wbbg.com

♥ Otters Pond Blueberry Stuffed French Toast ♥

12 slices French bread,
cut into 1" cubes
2 (8-ounce) pkgs. cream
cheese, chilled and cut
into 1/2" cubes
1 cup fresh blueberries,
rinsed & drained, or
frozen blueberries
12 large eggs
1/3 cup maple syrup
2 cups milk

Blueberry Syrup:
1 cup sugar
2 tablespoons
cornstarch
1 cup water
1 cup fresh blueberries,
rinsed & drained
1 tablespoon unsalted
butter

Grease a 9" x 13" baking pan. Place half of the bread cubes evenly in prepared pan. Scatter half the cream cheese cubes over bread and sprinkle with 1/2 cup blueberries. Arrange remaining bread cubes, cream cheese and blueberries. In large bowl combine eggs, maple syrup and milk and whisk to blend. Pour evenly over bread mixture. Cover with foil and chill overnight. Preheat oven to 350°. Bake, covered with foil, in middle of oven for 30 minutes. Remove foil and continue baking for 30 minutes, or until puffed and golden brown. For Syrup: In small saucepan combine sugar, cornstarch and water over medium-high heat. Cook, stirring occasionally, for 5 minutes or until thickened. Stir in blueberries and simmer, stirring occasionally, for 10 minutes or until most berries burst. Add butter and stir until melted. (May be prepared up to 1 day in advance. Chill and reheat gently.) Transfer to serving bowl. Place French toast on individual serving plates and top with Blueberry Syrup. Makes 8 - 10 servings. Great for a group!

Submitted by Otters Pond B&B of Orcas Island, Orcas Island

♥ Peach Pecan French Toast ♥

1 (12-ounce) loaf French bread, cut in 1" slices
1 (16-ounce) can peaches, sliced
6 large eggs

1 1/2 cups milk
1/2 cup half and half
2 teaspoons vanilla
1/2 teaspoon nutmeg
1/2 teaspoon cinnamon

Topping:

3/4 cup margarine, softened
1 1/3 cups brown sugar

3 tablespoons dark corn syrup
1 1/3 cups coarsely chopped pecans

Spray 9" x 13" baking pan with nonstick spray. Fill pan with a layer of bread slices. Place a layer of sliced peaches on top of each slice of bread. Place second layer of bread on top of the peach layer. Add second layer of peaches, if desired. Set aside. In blender mix eggs, milk, half and half, vanilla and spices. Pour mixture over bread, cover with plastic wrap and refrigerate overnight. Just before baking, make topping by mixing ingredients together, and spread evenly over the top. Bake at 350° for 50 minutes or until puffed and golden brown. Makes 6 - 8 servings.

Submitted by DeVoe Mansion, Tacoma

www.wbbg.com

♥ # Trumpeter Inn French Toast ♥

5 slices bread, cut 3/4" thick	1 cup brown sugar
5 eggs	1/2 cup butter
1 1/2 cups milk	2 tablespoons corn syrup
1 teaspoon vanilla	2 Granny Smith apples, peeled & sliced

Place bread slices in 10" x 13" pan. Mix eggs, milk, and vanilla together; pour over bread and refrigerate overnight. Combine brown sugar, butter, and corn syrup in pan and cook to boiling. Remove bread and pour syrup into pan. Cover with sliced apples and then bread slices. Bake uncovered at 350° for 40 minutes. Turn upside down to serve. Makes 5 servings.

Submitted by Trumpeter Inn B&B, San Juan Island

www.wbbg.com

Egg Dishes

Napkin Folding

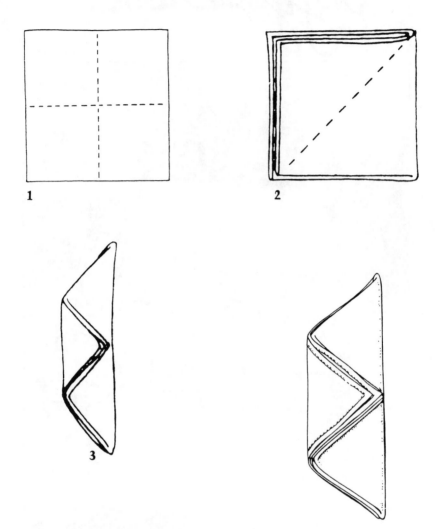

Simplesse

1. Fold the napkin in quarters.
2. Then fold it in half diagonally to form a triangle.
3. Place the folded edge on the right side, and fold left point over to the edge.

♥ Apple Country B&B Casserole ♥

2 pounds bulk sausage,
  cooked, grease reserved
2 apples, cored & sliced
9 slices bread, crusts
  removed and cubed

3/4 teaspoon dry mustard
9 eggs, beaten
1 1/2 cups grated sharp
  cheddar cheese
3 cups milk

Cook sausage, place in greased 9" x 13" baking dish. Sauté apple slices in reserved sausage grease. Combine apples, bread cubes, dry mustard, eggs, cheese and milk. Mix well and pour over sausage. Cover and refrigerate overnight. In the morning, heat oven to 350°. Bake covered for 30 minutes. Uncover and bake for another 30 minutes. Makes 12 servings.

Submitted by Apple Country B&B, Wenatchee

♥ Baked Confetti Eggs ♥

Shoestring potatoes to
  fill baking dish
1 egg

1/4 cup milk
Shredded sharp cheddar
  cheese, to taste

Butter 1 individual ramekin baking dish and fill with shoestring potatoes. Poke hole in center of potatoes with finger. Break egg on top of potatoes, and puncture yolk with toothpick. Pour milk on egg. Sprinkle cheese on top of egg. Cook in microwave on high for 1 minute and 20 seconds. Makes 1 serving.

Submitted by Old Brook Inn, Anacortes

♥   # Chili Brunch   ♥

12 eggs
1/3 cup all purpose flour
1 teaspoon garlic
  powder
1 teaspoon salt
1 teaspoon pepper

1 pound shredded
  cheddar cheese
2 cups cottage cheese
1 (4-ounce) can diced
  mild chilies
1/4 cup melted butter

Combine eggs, flour, garlic powder, salt, pepper, cheddar cheese, cottage cheese, and chilies in large pan. Add melted butter and mix well. Pour into greased 9" x 13" baking dish. Bake at 350° for about 45 minutes, until set and top is brown. Cool for 10 minutes; cut and serve. Can be refrigerated overnight before baking. Makes 12 servings.

Submitted by Hillside House B&B, San Juan Island

♥   # Cottage Cheese Delight   ♥

1 cup milk
1 cup flour
1 pint lowfat cottage
  cheese
1/2 cup melted butter or
  margarine

6 eggs
1 pound grated Monterey
  jack cheese
Bread crumbs or crushed
  leftover croissant
  crumbs, for topping

Blend first five ingredients together. Grease 8" or 9" square pan. Sprinkle cheese over the pan. Pour egg mixture over the cheese in the pan. Dust with bread crumbs. (I find this is a nice way to use up the leftover croissants from the day before. It adds a nice buttery, crunchy topping.) Bake at 350° for 45 minutes. Cut into squares and top with sour cream or vanilla yogurt, and fresh berries or fruit conserve. Makes 8 - 12 servings. Recipe may be doubled for 24 guests. Use a 9" x 13" pan and bake for 1 hour and 15 minutes, or until set and cracks appear in the center. It may be baked a day ahead and reheated on the serving plate in the oven or microwave. Leftovers make great blintzes as a filling in crepes. Top blintzes with sour cream and fruit also.

Submitted by Highland Inn of San Juan Island, Friday Harbor

♥ # Egg Bake ♥

1 pound bulk turkey
   sausage
10 large mushrooms,
   sliced
1 dozen eggs
1 can cream of mushroom
   soup

1 cup milk
Salt & pepper,
   to taste
Fresh rosemary,
   to taste
1 cup shredded sharp
   cheddar cheese

Brown sausage, drain on paper towels, and place in 9" x 13" baking pan. Layer with sliced mushrooms. Beat eggs. Mix eggs with soup, milk, salt, pepper, and fresh rosemary well. Pour over sausage and mushrooms. Sprinkle cheese over the top. Bake at 350° for 40 to 45 minutes. Makes 10 - 12 servings.

Submitted by The Fotheringham House, Spokane

www.wbbg.com

♥   **Egg, Spinach And Potato Delight**   ♥

1 large carrot, sliced in
    1/16" - 1/8" rounds
1 large (1 pound) baking
    potato, peeled & sliced
    in 1/16" - 1/8" rounds
1 medium onion, chopped
1 ounce butter
1 (10-ounce) pkg. frozen
    spinach, thawed

8 eggs
8 ounces shredded
    cheddar cheese,
    divided
1/2 teaspoon salt
1/4 teaspoon pepper
1/4 teaspoon freshly
    grated nutmeg

Butter the bottom and sides of a 7" soufflé dish. Slice carrot, parboil and drain. Peel potato, slice, parboil and drain. (If you get interrupted before you can boil the potatoes, place them in a bowl of cold water. Raw sliced potatoes will turn black if exposed to air.) Chop the onion. (If I have Walla Walla onions, I use a large onion.) Sauté the onion in butter until transparent. Let spinach set out of freezer for 15 minutes, then chop. Add spinach to onions; cook until spinach is heated. Beat together eggs, 4 ounces shredded cheddar cheese, salt, pepper and nutmeg. (Adjust seasonings to your taste.) Combine egg mixture with spinach and onions. Remove from heat. Eggs will not be cooked. Arrange half of the potatoes on the bottom of the dish. Pour in half of the egg mixture. Cover eggs with sliced carrots. Pour in remaining egg mixture. Top with remaining potatoes. Bake at 350° for 45 to 50 minutes. Add 4 ounces shredded cheddar cheese on top. Bake at 400° for 10 more minutes. Remove from oven and let rest for 20 to 30 minutes. Turn out onto a dinner plate and turn again, so that cheese is on top. Cut into 6 wedges and serve. Note: After assembly you may cover and refrigerate overnight. In the morning I put the cold dish in a cold oven, set the oven for 350° and bake for 1 hour and 20 minutes or until set. Then add cheese and bake for an additional 10 minutes. I serve this dish with baked Roma tomatoes. Cut tomatoes in half and sprinkle with salt, pepper, oregano, olive oil and Parmesan cheese. Bake or broil. Makes 6 servings.

Submitted by Olympic Lights, San Juan Island

♥ ## Never-Fail Bread & Cheese Strata ♥

6 slices cubed, dry
  bread
1 1/2 cups grated
  cheddar cheese
4 eggs
1 1/2 cups milk or cream

1/2 teaspoon dry
  mustard
1 teaspoon salt
Dash of pepper
Herbs of choice
1 tablespoon flour

Layer bread cubes and cheese into 4 greased ramekins. Blend together eggs, milk, seasonings, and flour; pour over top of bread. Bake at 375° for 30 minutes until puffed and lightly browned. May cover the last 15 minutes. Serve immediately. Makes 4 servings.

Submitted by The Duffy House B&B, Friday Harbor

♥ ## Scrambled Egg Casserole With ♥
Jalapenos & Sun-Dried Tomatoes

1/4 cup chopped sun-
  dried tomatoes
1 cup hot water
1/4 cup chopped
  jalapeno pepper
3 tablespoons butter
6 beaten eggs

1 tablespoon flour
1/8 teaspoon pepper
2/3 cup milk
3/4 cup shredded cheddar
  or Monterey jack cheese
1/4 cup seasoned bread
  crumbs

Soak tomatoes in hot water; set aside. Meanwhile in large skillet cook jalapeno pepper in 1 tablespoon butter. Add eggs; cook without stirring until they begin to set. Lift and fold so uncooked portion flows underneath. When set, transfer to 4 individual casseroles. In small saucepan melt 1 tablespoon butter; stir in flour and pepper. Add milk all at once. Cook and stir until thick and bubbly. Stir in cheese and tomatoes. Fold mixture into eggs. Melt 1 tablespoon butter, mix with bread crumbs and sprinkle on top. Bake at 350° for 20 to 25 minutes. To make ahead: Cover and refrigerate up to 24 hours. Bake an additional 10 minutes.

Submitted by Hummingbird Inn, Roslyn

♥ **Sunday Sausage Breakfast** ♥

6 ounces onion and
  garlic croutons
1 pound pork sausage,
  cooked & crumbled
2 cups cubed medium
  sharp cheddar
  cheese

2 cups cubed Monterey
  jack cheese
1 dozen eggs
1/2 cup milk
1/2 teaspoon dried basil
1/4 teaspoon salt
1/4 teaspoon pepper

Grease 9" x 13" pan. Layer croutons, sausage, cheddar cheese, and Monterey jack cheese. Mix eggs and milk; pour over the top of casserole. Mix together basil, salt, and pepper. Sprinkle seasonings over the top. Bake uncovered at 350° for 40 to 45 minutes.

Submitted by Angeles Inn, Port Angeles

♥ **Vegetable Egg Casserole** ♥

(crust)

1 2 cups Bisquick®
1/4 1/2 cup milk
4 8 eggs
1/2 red onion,
  chopped
1/2 cup grated Parmesan
  cheese

4 eggs
1 c. milk
1 1/2 cups shredded
  cheddar cheese
2 cups cottage cheese
1 teaspoon powdered
  garlic
1 cup cooked vegetables
  (spinach, broccoli, etc.)

Mix Bisquick®, milk, 4 eggs, and onion by hand in large bowl. Spread in bottom of greased 9" x 13" baking dish. Mix Parmesan cheese, 1 cup cheddar cheese, cottage cheese, remaining 4 eggs, garlic, and vegetables by hand in same bowl. Spread over Bisquick® mix. Sprinkle remaining 1/2 cup cheddar cheese over casserole. Bake at 350° for about 40 minutes, until done. Cheese should be slightly brown but don't let bottom burn. Can be refrigerated overnight before baking. Makes 14 servings.

Submitted by Hillside House B&B, San Juan Island

♥ # Artichoke Frittata ♥

1 (32-ounce) box frozen artichoke hearts (do not use marinated artichoke hearts)
1 pkg. frozen chopped onions (saves time & weeping)
2 1/2 cups half and half
12 eggs
1 tablespoon Worcestershire sauce
1 tablespoon Coleman's® mustard
2 teaspoons seasoning salt
3 sourdough English muffins, broken up
1 pound grated Monterey jack cheese
1/2 cup grated Parmesan cheese
1/2 cup seasoned Italian bread crumbs
Paprika, to taste
Parsley, to taste

Defrost artichoke hearts. Chop in blender or Cuisinart®. Coat a 9" x 13" pan with spray shortening and spread out the chopped artichoke hearts. Top with chopped onions. Blend half and half with eggs and seasonings. Pour half the egg mixture over artichokes and onions. Blend broken up English muffins with the remaining egg mixture until smooth. Pour this over artichoke mixture and stir to blend. Top with grated Monterey jack cheese, Parmesan cheese and bread crumbs. Sprinkle with a little paprika and parsley as desired. Bake at 350° for 1 hour and 15 minutes, or until set in the middle and cracks appear. Cool slightly and cut into 30 squares. It may be reheated in your serving dish in the microwave, or keep warm on low heat in the oven. Can be baked the day before and reheated. Nice served with fresh fruit, sausage or bacon and breads. Recipe may be halved or freeze half for smaller inns with fewer guests. This was developed for a 12-room inn. Makes 24 servings.

Submitted by Highland Inn of San Juan Island, Friday Harbor

♥ Hashbrown Frittata ♥

5 eggs
1/2 cup milk
3 cups thawed
  hashbrown potatoes
1/2 teaspoon salt
1/4 teaspoon Tabasco
  sauce
1/3 cup chopped green
  onions

2/3 cup chopped bacon,
  divided
1 1/2 cups shredded
  cheese, divided
Cherry tomato & kale
  for garnish
Salsa, Tabasco sauce
  & sour cream as
  accompaniments

Preheat oven to 350°. Beat eggs and milk. Add hashbrown potatoes, salt, 1/4 teaspoon Tabasco sauce and green onions. Stir in 1/3 cup chopped meat and 3/4 cup shredded cheese. Pour into greased pie dish and bake for 30 to 40 minutes. In last 5 minutes of baking, sprinkle top with another 1/3 cup chopped meat and 3/4 cup cheese. Garnish with cherry tomato and kale. Serve with salsa, Tabasco sauce and sour cream. Makes 6 servings.

Submitted by Campus View Inn, Ellensburg

♥ Greek Egg Casserole ♥

1 dozen eggs, beaten
1/3 cup milk
1/2 pound mushrooms,
  sliced
1 pkg. frozen spinach,
  thawed & drained
1 small onion,
  chopped

1 pkg. feta cheese,
  crumbled
1 teaspoon dill weed
1 teaspoon oregano
Shredded mozzarella,
  Monterey jack or other
  favorite cheese, to taste
Parsley

Spray large 9" x 13" oval casserole with nonstick cooking spray. Beat eggs, and add other ingredients, except shredded cheese and parsley. Pour into casserole. Sprinkle with shredded cheese, then with parsley. Bake at 350° for 40 minutes.

Submitted by Argyle House B&B, San Juan Island

♥ **Mexicali Eggs** ♥

8 eggs
1 cup Bisquick®
1 stick butter, melted
1 1/2 teaspoons cumin
1 (4-ounce) can green
  chilies, chopped

2 cups cottage cheese
2 cups shredded
  cheese
1 cup milk
1 (11-ounce) can of corn,
  without liquid

Preheat oven to 350°. Mix all ingredients well. Put in greased 9" x 13" baking pan. Bake for 45 to 50 minutes. Good with sour cream and salsa, accompanied by a crunchy toast.

Submitted by Chelsea Station on the Park, Seattle

Egg Substitutions:

Each of the following methods will work if you need to substitute the egg(s) called for in a recipe:

For each egg, substitute:
- *1/2 teaspoon baking powder, or*
- *1 tablespoon white vinegar, or*
- *2 tablespoons fresh apricot puree, or add*
- *An additional 1/2 cup of the liquid called for in the recipe*

Purchased Egg Substitute Products:
- *Use approximately 2 tablespoons of liquid product for each egg called for in the recipe*

♥ Moroccan Breakfast Pie ♥

1 1/2 cups toasted
  almonds
2 tablespoons sugar
2 teaspoons cinnamon
1 tablespoon butter
1 medium onion,
  chopped
1 clove garlic, minced
1/4 teaspoon ground
  ginger
1/4 teaspoon fresh ground
  pepper
1/4 teaspoon ground
  cumin
1/4 teaspoon ground
  coriander
1/4 teaspoon ground
  turmeric
1 teaspoon cinnamon
2 tablespoons fresh
  cilantro, chopped
1 tablespoon fresh
  parsley, chopped
10 large eggs
1/2 cup milk
1/2 pkg. phyllo pastry
  sheets
Nonstick cooking spray

Bake almonds at 375° for 7 minutes. Place in food processor and process with sugar and 2 teaspoons cinnamon until almost finely ground. Set aside. Sauté chopped onions in butter until tender. Add garlic, ginger, pepper, cumin, coriander, turmeric, and 1 teaspoon cinnamon. Stir until well blended; then add cilantro and parsley. Set aside. Scramble eggs with milk; cook until done. Set aside. Spray 9" x 9" Pyrex baking pan with nonstick cooking spray. Cut phyllo sheets in half. Layer six half sheets in pan, spraying after each sheet and dusting each evenly between sheets, using half of almond mixture. Spread onion mixture on top of almonds, then spread egg mixture on top of that. Repeat with six more sprayed phyllo half sheets, and almond layering, reserving 1/4 cup almond mixture for topping. Fold edges of phyllo over and cover top with two pleated sheets, add topping, spray, and sprinkle with almonds. Bake at 350° for 40 minutes. Makes 6 servings.

Submitted by Tower House B&B, San Juan Island

♥ Asparagus-Mushroom Omelet ♥

1 large egg
5 large egg whites
1 tablespoon chives
2 tablespoons cold water
1/4 teaspoon black
  pepper
2 tablespoons margarine

1/4 cup chopped, cooked
  asparagus
1/4 cup chopped
  mushrooms
1/4 cup finely chopped
  ripe tomato
1/4 cup minced parsley

Combine egg, egg whites, chives, water and pepper. Whisk just enough to mix lightly. Melt margarine in a heavy 7" skillet over moderately high heat. Add 1/4 each of the asparagus and mushrooms and cook for 1 minute. Add 1/4 of egg mixture, then let omelet cook, undisturbed, for 30 seconds. With a spatula, either fold the omelet in half or roll to the edge of the pan. Repeat to make 3 more omelets. Garnish with tomato and parsley. Makes 4 omelets.

Submitted by Glenna's Guthrie Cottage B&B, Sequim

♥ Cheddar & Chutney Omelet, French-Style ♥

3 tablespoons butter
1 small shallot, minced
1 medium green pepper,
  diced
1/2 small zucchini, thinly
  sliced

4 medium eggs, well
  beaten
1/2 teaspoon salt
1/4 teaspoon freshly
  ground black pepper
  or white pepper

Melt butter in 10" omelet pan and sauté vegetables until tender. Add well beaten eggs, stir, and permit bottom of mixture to brown. Turn out onto plate and immediately return to pan with uncooked side down. Or turn omelet over with large spatula. Cook second side until toothpick comes away clean from center. Makes 2 servings.

Submitted by Heaven's Edge B&B, Silverdale

♥Fresh Salmon Pesto Omelette With Mushrooms♥

Flaked salmon
Low sodium tamari
  sauce
Pesto (homemade
  is best)
Butter for frying

1 medium to large
  mushroom, diced/person
2 - 3 fresh eggs (we like
  brown eggs best)/person
Splash of milk

Make sure salmon is very fresh! Wash and debone, and coat with low sodium tamari sauce. Spread pesto on the fish. Broil salmon in oven just a few minutes until barely cooked through. Set aside. Can be cooked a day ahead, but will flake better if warm. Cut mushrooms into small pieces and lightly sauté in enough butter to keep from sticking. Set aside. Butter a good omelette pan on the bottom and up the sides to insure eggs won't stick and will brown well. Mix eggs and milk in blender on "Whip" until they stop rising. Assume an artistic attitude! Put 1/2" or less of egg into pan at a time. Cook on medium/high heat and as eggs begin to cook on the bottom, push in the edge and allow liquid to flow outward. When egg is partially cooked on the bottom, put in a light coating of flaked salmon and mushrooms on half of the eggs. Keep tending the edges until all liquid is lightly cooked. Flop the plain side over the other and take off the heat. Warm plates and serve with baked baby red potatoes, and a nasturtium or sunflower greens. Don't overcook!

Submitted by Angels of the Sea B&B, Vashon Island

♥ Herbed Yellow Pepper Omelet ♥ With Brie Cheese

5 large eggs, beaten
  lightly
1 1/2 teaspoons chopped
  fresh chives
1/4 teaspoon finely
  chopped fresh tarragon

1 tablespoon butter
1 yellow bell pepper,
  diced into 1/4" pieces
4 tablespoons Brie
  cheese, rind removed,
  cut into small chunks

In bowl whisk together eggs, chives, and tarragon. In nonstick skillet heat butter over moderate heat until foam subsides, and cook bell pepper, stirring until softened. Add eggs and lift edges of omelet as it cooks until almost set. Add Brie cheese, and heat through until cheese melts. Fold omelet over and cut in half. Makes 2 servings.

Submitted by Palisades B&B at Dash Point, Seattle / Tacoma

♥   # Oven Omelet   ♥

1/4 cup butter
18 eggs
1 cup sour cream
2 teaspoons salt
1 cup milk
1 bunch chopped
  green onions

1 cup cooked rice
1 can green chilies,
  chopped
1 teaspoon seasoning
  (garlic & basil mixture)
3/4 cup grated cheddar
  cheese

Heat oven to 325°, melting butter to coat dish. Beat eggs; add sour cream, salt, and milk. Stir in onions, cooked rice, green chilies, and seasoning. Pour mixture into dish, and bake until eggs start to set, then sprinkle cheese on top. Bake about 35 minutes, or until knife inserted comes out clean. Makes 12 - 15 servings.

Submitted by Mt. Higgins House, Darrington

♥   # Pan Omelet   ♥

1/2 loaf firm white bread
  (French bread), cut up
4 tablespoons butter,
  melted
1 cup grated Swiss
  cheese
2 cups diced ham
1 teaspoon dry mustard

3 tablespoons chopped
  green onion
1 1/2 cups milk
8 eggs
1/2 cup white wine
Salt & pepper, to taste
1 cup sour cream
1/2 cup Parmesan cheese

Mix together bread, butter, Swiss cheese, and ham; place in greased 9" x 13" pan. Mix together dry mustard, onion, milk, eggs, wine, salt, and pepper, and pour over bread mixture. Cover and place in refrigerator overnight. Bake at 375° for 45 minutes. Remove from oven and let stand for 30 minutes. Mix together sour cream and Parmesan cheese and spread on top of omelet. Broil until bubbly and golden in color. Enjoy! Makes 12 servings.

Submitted by Heaven's Edge B&B, Silverdale

♥ Salsa Omelette ♥

1/2 cup flour
1/4 teaspoon salt
1 teaspoon baking powder
10 eggs, slightly
  beaten
1/4 cup butter

2 (4-ounce) cans chopped
  green chilies
1 pint small curd
  cottage cheese
1 pound grated Monterey
  jack cheese

Add dry ingredients to eggs and mix. Add remaining ingredients and mix together. Grease a 9" x 13" x 2" pan. Bake at 350° for 45 to 50 minutes. Let stand for 5 to 7 minutes before cutting. Makes 10 - 11 servings.

Submitted by The Churchyard Inn, Uniontown

♥ Skagit Bay Crab And Havarti Omelet ♥

5 - 6 mushrooms, thinly
  sliced
2+ tablespoons butter
1/2 of a plum tomato,
  chopped
1 - 2 green onions,
  chopped

4 eggs
1 1/2 tablespoons
  cream
Havarti cheese, thinly
  sliced
1/8 pound fresh
  Dungeness crab

Sauté mushrooms in 2 tablespoons butter over low heat. Chop tomato and green onions. Melt additional butter in 10" omelet pan. Mix eggs and cream well, and pour into pan. Cook over low heat for 20 to 30 minutes. After eggs are set, place thin slices of Havarti cheese to cover omelet and let melt. Add crab, sautéed mushrooms, and most of tomato and green onions (reserve enough for garnish). Fold omelet in half and slide onto serving dish. Serve with garnish of tomatoes, green onions and fresh nasturtiums on top. Makes 1 omelet.

Submitted by Skagit Bay Hideaway, La Conner

♥ ## Cascade Mountain Inn Spinach Quiche ♥

1 (12-ounce) pkg.
  Stouffer's® spinach
  soufflé
1 deep-dish pie crust,
  pricked & baked
3/4 pound sausage,
  cooked & drained
1 cup sliced mushrooms

2 tablespoons chopped
  onion
2 tablespoons butter,
  melted
2 eggs, beaten
3 tablespoons milk
3/4 cup cheese

Prepare the spinach soufflé according to the directions on the package. Prick the pie crust all over and bake at 400° for 7 to 10 minutes. Brown the sausage and pour off the fat. Sauté the mushrooms and onion in butter; combine with the beaten eggs and milk. Mix with the soufflé and pour into the crust. Arrange the cheese and sausage on top. Bake at 400° for 25 to 30 minutes. Let stand for 5 minutes before slicing. Note: Use pork sausage with cheddar cheese. Use Italian sausage with mozzarella cheese. Makes 6 servings.

Submitted by Cascade Mountain Inn, Concrete-Birdsview

♥ ## Cheese Quiche ♥

4 eggs, beaten
1/2 cup butter, melted
  in microwave
1/2 cup buttermilk
  baking mix

1 1/2 cups milk
1/2 cup medium cheddar
  cheese, grated
1/2 cup Monterey jack
  cheese, grated

Preheat oven to 350°. Beat ingredients together with a wire whisk and pour into a glass pie plate. Bake for 45 minutes. Cool for 5 minutes before cutting into wedges. Makes 6 - 8 servings.

Submitted by A Harbor View B&B, Aberdeen

♥   **Crustless Spinach Quiche**   ♥

1 large onion, chopped
2 cloves garlic, chopped
1/2 red pepper, chopped
3 tablespoons jicama,
  chopped
Olive oil
6 eggs (or Egg
  Beaters®)

1 cup skim milk
1/8 teaspoon nutmeg
1/8 teaspoon pepper
1 (10-ounce) pkg.
  chopped spinach,
  thawed & drained well
1 cup grated Swiss
  cheese

Sauté onion, garlic, red pepper, and jicama in olive oil until soft. Combine with remainder of ingredients. Spray 8" x 8" baking dish with Pam® nonstick cooking spray. Pour mixture into dish. Bake at 350° for 40 minutes or until silver knife inserted in center comes out clean.

Submitted by Reflections B&B, Port Orchard

♥   **Crustless Spinach-Cheese Quiche**   ♥

4 eggs, beaten
1 teaspoon onion powder
1 cup+ sour cream
1 cup small curd
  cottage cheese
1/4 cup Bisquick®

1 cup shredded
  mozzarella cheese
2 cups shredded Monterey
  jack cheese
5 ounces drained,
  chopped spinach

Beat eggs; mix in onion powder, sour cream, cottage cheese, Bisquick®, mozzarella cheese, and Monterey jack cheese. Thaw a 10 ounce box of chopped spinach. Drain half the box well on paper towels. Mix in with egg-cheese mixture. Divide mixture into 8 greased custard cups, placed on a cookie sheet. Bake at 350° for 30 minutes in convection oven, 40 to 60 minutes in conventional oven. Let stand for 5 minutes before turning out onto serving plate. Garnish with 1/2 teaspoon sour cream and parsley.

Submitted by Katy's Inn, La Conner

♥ ## Fresh Salmon Quiche ♥

2 tablespoons butter
1/2 teaspoon fresh dill
Juice of 1/2 lemon
Squirt of Worcestershire
 sauce
6 1/2 ounces fresh
 skinned salmon
1 tablespoon butter,
 spread in 1 pie crust
2 cups whipping cream
 or half and half

4 eggs or Egg Beaters®
1/2 teaspoon salt
1/4 pound grated dill
 Havarti cheese
2 tablespoons butter
2 tablespoons chopped
 green onions
6 sliced mushrooms
1 teaspoon fresh dill
1/8 teaspoon fresh
 ground pepper

Preheat electric oven to 350° or convection oven to 325°. Melt 2 tablespoons butter and add 1/2 teaspoon fresh dill, lemon juice and Worcestershire sauce. Spread with brush over salmon and bake for 20 minutes. Let cool and flake off into large pieces. Spread 1 tablespoon butter in pie crust. Mix whipping cream or half and half, eggs or Egg Beaters® and 1/2 teaspoon salt until well blended. Stir in grated dill Havarti cheese and set aside. In 1-quart sauté pan melt 2 tablespoons butter. Add green onions and mushrooms and cook until tender. Add to cream mixture. Add 1 teaspoon fresh dill and fresh ground pepper. Pour into pie crust. Bake in electric oven at 425° for 15 minutes, then at 325° for 35 minutes. Bake in convection oven at 400° for 15 minutes and at 300° for 35 minutes. Quiche is ready when knife inserted in center comes out clean.

Submitted by The Green Cape Cod B&B, Tacoma

www.wbbg.com

♥ Garden Quiche ♥

10 eggs
1/2 cup flour
1 teaspoon baking
  powder
2 ounces melted butter
3 cups cottage cheese
12 ounces shredded
  Monterey jack or
  cheddar cheese (or
  combination of both)

1 (10-ounce) pkg. frozen
  spinach, thawed &
  squeezed dry
1 large red or yellow
  pepper, chopped
1 medium yellow onion,
  chopped
1 teaspoon dry thyme or
  1 tablespoon fresh
  minced thyme

Beat together eggs, flour, baking powder, and melted butter. Stir in cottage cheese, shredded cheese, drained spinach, and red or yellow pepper. (Broil pepper until most of the skin is charred. Let cool in a paper bag for about 15 minutes. Then remove skin, stem, and seeds. Chop pepper.) Sauté onion. When almost done, add thyme. Add to other ingredients. Pour into 2 pie plates or 12 - 6 ounce baking dishes sprayed with nonstick cooking spray. Bake at 350° for 40 minutes. Makes 12 servings.

Submitted by Olympic Lights, San Juan Island

♥ Green Chilies/Cream Cheese Quiche ♥

2 - 9" pie crusts, baked
6 beaten eggs
2 1/2 cups milk
1/2 teaspoon salt
8 ounces cream
  cheese

3 cups grated Monterey
  jack cheese
2 tablespoons flour
1 (4-ounce) can diced
  green chilies, drained
Dash of nutmeg

Prepare pastry for two single crust pies. (I use Pillsbury® prepared crusts.) Bake crusts until lightly brown. Blend eggs, milk, and salt in blender. Add cream cheese and blend lightly so that there are small chunks of cream cheese left in mixture. Mix grated Monterey jack cheese and flour together and add to milk mixture. Drain green chilies on paper towel. Dice and add to mixture; mix well. Pour into prepared pastry shells. Dust tops with nutmeg. Bake at 325° for approximately 45 minutes or until knife inserted in center comes out clean. Cool for 15 minutes before serving. Makes 12 servings.

Submitted by Green Gables Inn, Walla Walla

♥ # Mushroom Quiche ♥

Crust:

1 stick butter
1 cup flour

2 - 3 tablespoons ice
  cold water

Filling:

2 tablespoons butter
1 tablespoon olive oil
2 cups mushrooms,
  trimmed & sliced
1 tablespoon garlic,
  chopped

Juice of 1/2 lemon
Salt & pepper, to taste
Fresh parsley, to taste
3 - 4 eggs
1 1/2 cups half and half
1/2 cup Parmesan cheese

For crust: Cream together butter and flour. Add cold water until mixture holds and is not dry. Refrigerate for 2 to 3 hours. Press into 10" tart or pie pan. Bake at 375° for 15 minutes or until golden. Prepare filling while baking crust. Heat butter and olive oil in skillet. Sauté mushrooms, garlic, lemon juice, salt and pepper until mushrooms release liquid and it evaporates. Add parsley and remove from heat. In bowl whisk together eggs and half and half. Add mushroom mixture. In baked pie shell sprinkle Parmesan cheese. Pour in egg mixture and bake at 375° for 15 to 30 minutes. Makes 6 servings.

Submitted by Angelica's B&B, Spokane

♥ # Shrimp & Crab Quiche ♥

1 - 8" unbaked pie crust
2 tablespoons butter
1/2 cup chopped onion
3 eggs, beaten
3/4 cup light cream
3/4 cup milk
1/2 teaspoon salt
1/2 teaspoon lemon peel

1/8 teaspoon nutmeg
1 tablespoon flour
1 1/2 cups grated Swiss
  cheese
4 ounces crab meat
4 ounces bay cooked
  shrimp
1/4 cup sliced almonds

Preheat oven to 350°. Bake pie crust for 8 minutes and remove from oven. Melt butter in skillet. Sauté chopped onion. Mix in a bowl eggs, cream, milk, sautéed onion, salt, lemon peel, nutmeg, flour and grated cheese. Add seafood and almonds. Pour mixture into the pie crust. Bake at 350° for 45 minutes.

Submitted by Angeles Inn, Port Angeles

♥   # Smoked Salmon Quiche   ♥

4 eggs + 1 egg yolk,
  beaten
1/2 cup butter,
  melted
1/2 cup baking mix
1 1/2 cups milk

1/2 cup sharp cheddar
  cheese, grated
1/2 cup Swiss cheese,
  grated
3/4 cup smoked salmon,
  flaked

Preheat oven to 350°. Butter 9" or 10" pie pan. Mix eggs, melted butter, baking mix, and milk. Whisk smooth. Pour into pie pan. Dot egg mixture with grated cheeses and flaked salmon, pressing into egg mixture, if necessary, to submerge. Bake for 45 minutes. Cut into wedges to serve.

Submitted by Foxbridge B&B, Poulsbo

♥   # Cottage Soufflés   ♥

6 farm eggs
1/4 teaspoon onion
  powder
1/4 teaspoon garlic
  powder
1/4 teaspoon salt
1/4 teaspoon coarse
  ground pepper
1/2 teaspoon dry mustard

1 dash of Tabasco sauce
1/2 cup cottage
  cheese
1/2 cup shredded
  cheddar cheese
1/2 cup shredded
  Monterey jack cheese
Chopped fresh chives
  for garnish

Beat the eggs with a wire whisk until smooth. Whisk in the spices, except chives. Add cottage cheese. Stir in the cheddar and jack cheeses. Place 6 well greased small ramekins on a cookie sheet. Fill them with egg mixture up to 1/4" from top. Sprinkle chopped chives on top and bake at 350° for 30 minutes. Makes 6 soufflés.

Submitted by Edenwild Inn, Lopez Island

♥ Little Egg Soufflés ♥

2 eggs, beaten
1 tablespoon sour
  cream
1/2 teaspoon baking
  powder

Dash of herbs
1 teaspoon water
4 - 5 drops hot sauce
1/2 cup shredded
  cheddar cheese

Combine all ingredients except shredded cheese. Mix well. Stir in cheese. Pour into 2 greased 6-ounce custard cups or individual soufflé dishes. Bake at 350° for 12 to 14 minutes or until set. Makes 2 servings.

Submitted by Tudor Inn, Port Angeles

♥ Potatoes Cheese Soufflé ♥

4 large eggs
1 teaspoon water
Dash of salt

1/4 cup shredded medium
  cheddar cheese
10 mini tater tots

Beat eggs, water and salt together. Add cheese and tater tots. Spray 2 (1-cup) ramekins with vegetable spray. Divide mixture between the two ramekins. Bake at 350° for 25 minutes. May be served with salsa if desired.

Submitted by Soundview B&B, Seattle

♥   **Three Mushroom Soufflé**

5 eggs, separated
3 tablespoons butter
1/4 cup minced green
  onion
Dash of cayenne
  pepper
1/4 teaspoon dry mustard
1/8 teaspoon ground
  nutmeg
1 tablespoon dried
  tarragon

1/2 teaspoon salt
8 ounces mushrooms (4
  oz. button, 2 oz. portabello, & 2 oz. shiitake,
  all finely chopped)
3 tablespoons flour
1/2 cup milk
1/3 cup grated Romano
  cheese
1/4 cup chopped
  parsley for garnish

Preheat oven to 350°. Separate eggs, set aside. In 2 quart saucepan cook butter, onions, and spices over medium/high heat. Add mushrooms; cook until condensed. Add flour to form base. Add milk, stir until thickened. Add Romano cheese. Remove from heat and stir in egg yolks one at a time. Set aside. Do not heat after egg yolks have been added. Beat egg whites until stiff but not dry, just until they peak. Add 1/3 of egg whites to hot mixture in saucepan and stir together. Add sauce to remainder of egg whites and fold until mixed. Spray individual 4" soufflé dishes with nonstick cooking spray. Fill 3/4 full. Place on tray and bake on center rack of oven. Bake for 25 to 30 minutes. Garnish with parsley. Serve immediately. Makes 4 - 5 servings.

Submitted by Eagles Nest Inn, Whidbey Island - Langley

♥   **Barnum Point Crab Special**   ♥

1 tablespoon chopped
  green pepper
1 tablespoon chopped
  onion
2 - 3 eggs
1 tablespoon milk

1/8 cup+ fresh or frozen
  crab, cracked & shelled
2 thin slices cheddar
  cheese
1 teaspoon lemon-dill
  seasoning

Soften pepper and onion in 5" microwave-safe bowl on high for about 1 minute. Add eggs and milk and mix. Microwave for approximately 1 minute per egg until almost set. Check eggs and stir at least once. Spread warmed crab (you may use more than 1/8 cup if desired) and cheese slices on top. Sprinkle with seasoning and broil or heat until cheese melts.

Submitted by Inn at Barnum Point, Camano Island

♥ Breakfast Pinwheels ♥

6 eggs
1/2 cup cream
Salt & white pepper,
  to taste
Parmesan cheese, to taste
2 cups broccoli
  flowerets
1 cup slivered mushrooms
Garlic, to taste

Salt & pepper, to taste
1 cup sour cream
1 cup shredded white
  cheese
2 tablespoons butter
2 tablespoons flour
Milk, as needed
Shredded sharp cheddar
  cheese, to taste

Mix eggs, cream, salt, and white pepper. Pour into greased 9" x 13" baking dish. Bake at 350° for 20 to 30 minutes. Carefully slip out onto waxed paper covered with Parmesan cheese. Pre-cook broccoli, mushrooms, garlic, salt, and pepper until tender. Layer sour cream, white cheese, and broccoli and mushroom mix onto eggs. Roll into a log and slice into medallions. Mix butter, flour, milk, and cheese together in saucepan on medium heat, stirring until smooth. Pour cheese sauce onto serving plate; place medallions in center. Garnish and serve.

Submitted by Inn at Barnum Point, Camano Island

♥ Canadian Bacon Parmesan Eggs ♥

1 slice Canadian bacon
1 egg
1 tablespoon whipping
  cream

1 tablespoon Parmesan
  cheese
Dill, to taste

Spray an individual ramekin cup with nonstick cooking spray. Place Canadian bacon in bottom of cup. Break egg on top of bacon, followed by whipping cream, and then Parmesan cheese. Garnish top with dill. Bake at 350° for 12 to 15 minutes (or until edges just start to turn light brown). Using rubber spatula, loosen all edges and remove from cup. Makes 1 serving.

Submitted by DeVoe Mansion, Tacoma

♥ # Eggs Benedict ♥

4 English muffins,
  split into halves
8 slices Canadian-style
  bacon
8 eggs, poached in water
1/4 cup butter
1/4 cup flour
1 teaspoon paprika
1/8 teaspoon nutmeg

1/8 teaspoon pepper
2 cups milk
2 cups shredded Swiss
  cheese
1/4 cup white wine
1/2 cup crushed Corn
  Flakes® cereal
1 tablespoon melted
  butter

Arrange split and toasted muffins in greased 9" x 13" baking dish. Place one slice Canadian bacon on each muffin half. Half fill a 10" skillet with water; bring just to boiling. Break one egg into a dish. Carefully slide egg into water. Repeat with three more eggs. Simmer uncovered for 3 minutes; remove with slotted spoon. Repeat with remaining eggs. Place one egg on top of each bacon round; set aside. In medium saucepan melt 1/4 cup butter. Stir in flour, paprika, nutmeg, and pepper. Add milk all at once. Cook and stir until thick and bubbly. Stir in cheese until melted. Stir in wine. Spoon sauce over muffin stacks. Combine Corn Flakes® and 1 tablespoon melted butter, and sprinkle over muffin stacks. Cover and chill overnight. Bake, uncovered, at 375° for 20 to 25 minutes.

Submitted by The Guest House B&B, Seattle

www.wbbg.com

♥ ## Mushroomed Eggs In Lemon Sauce ♥

12 - 16 eggs, scrambled
Salt & pepper, to taste
1 pound mushrooms,
  sliced
2 tablespoons minced
  shallots or green onions
7 tablespoons butter
1 cup grated Parmesan or
  Parmesan, cheddar, &
  Swiss mixture

Lemon Sauce:
5 tablespoons butter
6 tablespoons flour
2 cups milk
1 cup heavy cream or
  half and half
Salt & pepper, to taste
1 teaspoon lemon juice
  or 1/4 teaspoon lemon
  extract

Scramble eggs with salt and pepper in 4 tablespoons butter until softly done. Remove to greased or buttered 9" x 13" glass baking dish. Sauté mushrooms and onions in remaining 3 tablespoons butter until lightly done. Spread mixture evenly over egg mixture and sprinkle with about 1/3 of cheese. For Lemon Sauce: Melt 5 tablespoons butter in same large frying pan used for eggs and onions. Blend flour, and cook until bubbly, stirring constantly. Gradually add in a little milk, on low heat, until mixture is smooth. Continue to whisk in remaining milk. Whisk in cream, salt, and pepper, and simmer for 4 to 5 minutes, until smooth and creamy. Beat in lemon juice. Pour sauce over eggs and mushrooms and top with remaining cheese. You may cover with foil and refrigerate overnight. Bake at 375° for 15 to 20 minutes. If refrigerated, bring dish to room temperature before baking. Serve over toasted, buttered English muffins. Garnish with fresh parsley and slivered olives. Makes 6 - 10 servings.

Submitted by Ravenscroft Inn, Port Townsend

www.wbbg.com

♥ ## Potato Boats With Eggs ♥

2 medium baking potatoes
Melted butter
Salt & pepper, to taste
6 eggs
2 green onions, chopped

1/8 teaspoon dill
1/4 cup smoked salmon
  pieces
3 dollops sour cream
Paprika

Wash potatoes and bake at 450° for 45 minutes. Slice potatoes in half and scoop out inside, leaving 1/4" of potato. Brush insides of potato halves with melted butter. Sprinkle with salt and pepper, to taste. Refrigerate until morning. In the morning, bake potato boats at 450° for 10 minutes, or until hot. While boats bake, beat eggs. Add onion, dill, salt, pepper and salmon pieces. Pour into a lightly oiled skillet and scramble over medium heat. When almost set, add sour cream. Remove boats from oven and fill with scrambled eggs mixture. Sprinkle with paprika and serve. Makes 4 servings.

Submitted by The Log Castle B&B, Whidbey Island - Langley

♥ ## Smoked Salmon or Herb Cheese Egg Puff ♥

9 eggs
1/2 cup milk
6 ounces cream cheese
1/4 cup butter, melted
1/2 teaspoon salt

1/4 teaspoon pepper
Sprinkle of dried dill
1/4 cup smoked salmon
Dill & paprika for
  topping

In large bowl combine eggs, milk, cream cheese, melted butter, and seasonings. Use a potato masher to mix. Put flaked smoked salmon into individual Pam®-sprayed ramekins. Pour egg mixture into ramekins and mix gently with smoked salmon. Sprinkle dill and paprika on top. Bake at 350° for 15 to 18 minutes until firm in center and puffed. Makes 4 servings. Plan on 2+ eggs per serving. (8 servings is about 1 1/2 times this recipe). For Herb Cheese Egg Puff: Put 4 or 5 half teaspoons full soft Brie herb cheese into each of 4 or 5 ramekins. Pour egg mixture over and cook for 15 minutes or until puffed.

Submitted by Otters Pond B&B of Orcas Island, Orcas Island

♥ # Vegetable Souttata ♥

8 eggs
1 1/4 - 1 1/2 cups milk
Salt & pepper, to taste
Pinch of dried oregano
  or basil or 1 tablespoon
  fresh rosemary
1/4 red bell pepper,
  diced

2 green onions,
  chopped
2 mushrooms, finely
  sliced
Dry Parmesan cheese
3 - 4 ounces grated sharp
  cheddar cheese

Preheat oven to 450°. In mixing bowl blend eggs, milk, salt, pepper, and oregano or basil or rosemary well. Set aside prepared bell pepper, onions, and mushrooms. Spray 4 - 6 ounce oven safe custard cups with nonstick cooking spray and coat lightly with dry Parmesan cheese. Pour egg mixture into cups to within 1/2" of cup rim. Divide pepper, onion, and mushroom mixture and cheddar cheese evenly into 4 servings and add to each cup, adding cheese last. Stir gently to mix vegetables and cheese into egg mixture. Place cups on a cookie sheet and bake on middle oven rack for 18 to 20 minutes. Souttatas are done when lightly browned with rounded top, having risen half again in height similar to a soufflé. Serve immediately. This delicious dish serves well with fresh fruit and sautéed baby red potatoes. Serves 4.

Submitted by Chelsea Station on the Park, Seattle

♥ # Veggie Benedict ♥

4 potatoes, diced
Salt, pepper and dry
  basil, to taste
1 - 2 tablespoons
  olive oil
1/2 green pepper, thinly
  sliced
1/2 red or orange pepper,
  thinly sliced

1/2 yellow pepper,
  thinly sliced
3/4 cup sliced
  mushrooms
3 green onions,
  sliced
Hollandaise sauce
4 eggs, poached
Paprika & parsley/garnish

Sprinkle salt, pepper and basil on potatoes, then sauté in oil for approximately 20 minutes, over medium heat. Add remaining vegetables and sauté until tender crisp. Make your favorite Hollandaise sauce and poach eggs. Divide vegetables between four plates, place a poached egg on each and top with sauce. Garnish with paprika and parsley. I also decorate plate with fresh fruit and flowers.

Submitted by Stratford Manor, Bellingham

♥   # WindSong Egg Rollade   ♥

1 bunch scallions,
  thinly sliced
1 cup basil, fresh and
  chiffonaded
6 large eggs
2 cups heavy cream
1/2 teaspoon salt

1 dash Tabasco sauce
2 tablespoons butter
3 ounces cream cheese,
  diced
2 cups corn kernels,
  defrosted
Tomato coulis/topping

Preheat oven to 325°. Reserve scallions and basil separately. Butter bottom and sides of jelly roll pan (15" x 10") and one side of parchment paper. Cover sides and bottom of pan with buttered parchment paper. Whip eggs and add heavy cream to combine. Add salt and Tabasco sauce. Pour into parchment paper and bake for 9 minutes, turning 180° after 8 minutes. Melt butter over medium heat. Add reserved scallions and sauté for 3 minutes. Add cream cheese and corn and cook for another 4 minutes. Remove egg custard from oven after baking for 17 minutes. Make sure that custard will lift off of parchment when rolling. Spread scallion mixture on top of custard. Spread basil on top of scallion mixture, covering the egg custard as much as possible. Using the parchment paper, roll the egg custard. Cut into serving pieces and top with tomato coulis. Note: Fresh herbs may be substituted for basil and chevre for cream cheese. A light, fresh tomato sauce is my definition of "coulis."

Submitted by WindSong Inn, Orcas Island, San Juan Islands

www.wbbg.com

Accompaniments

Melissa Pigg ©

Napkin Folding

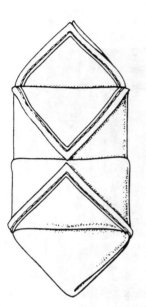

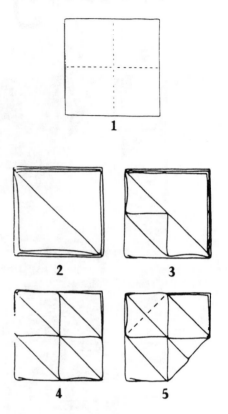

Hexagon Fold

1. Fold the napkin in quarters.
2. Place it so the free corners are at the upper right. Take the top right corner of the first layer and fold to the lower left corner.
3. Fold corner point toward the center diagonal fold.
4. Repeat as illustrated.
5. Fold the bottom right and top left corners under.

♥ **Chelsea Station Smoked Salmon Hash** ♥

Potato wedges, tossed
 with olive oil and
 liberally salted, roasted
6 ounces smoked salmon,
 cut into strips
1/2 cup finely chopped
 red onions
1 tablespoon drained
 capers

3 tablespoons sour cream
2 tablespoons prepared
 horseradish
1 tablespoon brown
 mustard
Salt & pepper, to taste
4 poached eggs
Lemon slices & fresh
 rosemary for garnish

Roast a large cookie sheet full of potato wedges tossed with olive oil and liberally salted at 450° for 20 to 25 minutes, depending on size. Prepare and mix together salmon, onions, capers, sour cream, horseradish and brown mustard. Place roasted potatoes in large skillet and continue to brown. Stir in half of salmon mixture and cook just until heated through, for about 2 minutes. Season with salt and pepper, to taste. Divide into four servings and top with remaining salmon mixture and a poached egg. Garnish with lemon slices and fresh rosemary sprig. Makes 4 servings.

Submitted by Chelsea Station on the Park, Seattle

♥ **Salmon Breakfast Pizza** ♥

1 Boboli® or similar
 pizza shell
8 ounces cream cheese
Garlic, to taste
Salt & pepper, to taste
1/2 cup chopped cilantro
1/4 cup mayonnaise
Juice of half a lime, and
 its zest

1/3 pound smoked
 salmon, flaked
1 cucumber, thinly
 sliced
2 red, green, or yellow
 peppers, thinly sliced
3 - 4 Roma tomatoes,
 thinly sliced
2 cups shredded cheese

Crisp pizza shell in 400° oven for 5 to 10 minutes. Let cool. Mix cream cheese until fluffy. Add garlic, salt, pepper, cilantro, and mayonnaise. Mix well. Add lime juice and zest. Mix until desired spreading consistency. Spread on cooled pizza shell. Place small mound of smoked salmon in center; surround with cucumber slices, add a ring of smoked salmon, surround with peppers, add another ring of salmon, surround with tomato slices. Top with shredded cheese. Bake at 400° for 10 to 15 minutes, until cheese melts and is bubbly. This is great served with fresh fruit and popovers.

Submitted by South Bay B&B, Lake Whatcom - Sedro Woolley

♥ Smoked Salmon Hash ♥

1 1/3 pounds russet or Idaho potatoes, peeled & sliced
Boiling water
2 tablespoons unsalted butter
1 tablespoon vegetable oil
1 large clove garlic, minced
1/2 cup minced onion
1/3 cup finely chopped celery
2 tablespoons chopped pimento
2 tablespoons diced green pepper
6 tablespoons cream or milk
1/4 teaspoon ground pepper
1/4 cup minced fresh parsley
10 ounces smoked salmon, with skin, gray fat & bones removed

Cook sliced potato in boiling water until just tender, 5 to 6 minutes. Drain, rinse under cold water, and pat dry. In heavy 8" skillet over high heat melt 1 tablespoon butter with 1 tablespoon oil. Add potatoes and cook until crisp and golden, 2 to 3 minutes, stirring frequently. Transfer potatoes to medium bowl and set aside. In same skillet, over medium-low heat, melt 1 tablespoon butter. Add garlic, onion, celery, pimento, and green pepper. Cook until soft, about 6 minutes, stirring occasionally. Add this mixture to potatoes. Stir cream and pepper into potatoes. Cool to room temperature. Mix parsley and cubed salmon into potatoes. Taste, and add salt if needed. Cover and refrigerate for up to 24 hours if made ahead. Before serving, bake at 350° or in microwave until hot. To serve, put scrambled eggs in center of serving dish; then arrange smoked salmon hash around eggs. Makes 4 servings.

Submitted by Peacock Hill Guest House, Gig Harbor Area

♥ ## Whalebone Hash ♥

2 pounds red potatoes
1 pound smoked salmon
1 small red onion,
  chopped fine
1 - 2 tablespoons
  prepared horseradish,
  or to taste
1 tablespoon coarse-
  grained mustard

1/4 cup capers
1/4 cup sour cream
Salt, black pepper and
  cayenne pepper, to taste
2 tablespoons butter
2 tablespoons vegetable
  oil
Additional sour cream
  and heavy cream

The night before place potatoes in a large pan and cover with water. Bring to a boil, cooking until tender when pierced with a knife. Place in the refrigerator overnight. Prep for cooking by peeling and cubing. Shred smoked salmon (making sure bones are removed) and place in medium bowl. Add onion, horseradish, mustard, capers and 1/4 cup sour cream. Toss to combine. Add salt, black pepper and cayenne pepper, to taste. In large skillet over medium high heat, melt butter and add oil (or substitute 4 tablespoons bacon fat for butter and oil). Add cubed potatoes and cook until golden brown and crisp. Salt and pepper, to taste. Add salmon mixture and toss to combine and heat through. Divide among 4 plates and garnish with a little sour cream that has been thinned with cream. Makes 4 servings.

Submitted by The Whalebone House,
Ocean Park - Long Beach Peninsula

www.wbbg.com

♥ Broiled Brown Sugar Apples With Bacon ♥

2 McIntosh apples,
  cored & sliced
3 tablespoons light
  brown sugar

1/4 pound sliced bacon,
  (about 4 slices) cooked
  crisply & chopped

Preheat broiler. Cut apples crosswise into 1/3" thick slices. Cut out core and arrange slices on a 15 1/2" x 10 1/2" jelly roll pan, keeping slices in order for restacking. Sprinkle with brown sugar. Broil 4" - 6" from heat for 2 minutes, until sugar is caramelized. Preheat oven to 350°. Lightly grease small, shallow baking dish. Arrange chopped bacon on top of each apple slice and then stack apples in order, ending with top slices of apples, to form 2 whole apples again. Reheat apples, uncovered, in oven until hot, about 15 minutes. Makes 2 servings.

Submitted by Palisades B&B at Dash Point, Seattle / Tacoma

♥ Company Bacon ♥

1 pound sliced bacon
1/3 cup brown sugar

1 1/2 tablespoons mustard
1 teaspoon honey

Heat oven to 350°. Spray broiler pan with Pam® nonstick cooking spray. Lay single layer of bacon in pan. Mix brown sugar, mustard, and honey to make a smooth sauce. Spread lightly on bacon. Bake for 15 minutes. Check. Continue baking until done, checking frequently.

Submitted by Foxbridge B&B, Poulsbo

♥ Homemade Italian Sausage ♥

1 pound ground pork
2 teaspoons fennel seeds
1/2 teaspoon chili
  garlic sauce

1 teaspoon garlic
  powder
1/4 teaspoon pepper
1 teaspoon salt

Mix all items well. Refrigerate overnight. Shape into patties or crumbles. Cook until completely done.

Submitted by Childs' House B&B, Olalla

♥ # Mom's Ham Loaves ♥

2 1/2 pounds smoked ground ham
2 pounds ground pork
1 pound lean ground beef
3 beaten eggs
2 cups milk

3 cups graham cracker crumbs
Sauce:
2 cans tomato soup
3/4 cup vinegar
1 1/2 - 2 cups sugar
2 teaspoons dry mustard

Have butcher grind together ham, pork, and beef. Combine eggs and milk, add to meat mixture and mix well (will be sloppy). Add graham cracker crumbs and combine. I use a large bowl and I use my hands! Use 1/2 cup measuring cup to measure meat loaves. Form in small ovals and place on baking rack. Bake at 350° for 45 to 60 minutes. For Sauce: Combine all ingredients in saucepan, but do not cook. Let stand while loaves bake. When ready to serve, heat sauce and pour over loaves. Loaves can be frozen before baking - add 15 minutes to baking time.

Submitted by South Bay B&B, Lake Whatcom - Sedro Woolley

♥ # Polynesian Sausage ♥

2 tablespoons salad oil
1/4 cup chopped onion
1/4 cup chopped celery
1 green pepper, chopped
1/2 teaspoon paprika
1/2 teaspoon salt
1 dash Tabasco sauce
1 tablespoon Worcester-shire sauce

Juice of half a lemon
1/4 cup brown sugar
1 tablespoon prepared mustard
1/4 cup cider vinegar
1 (12-ounce) bottle chili sauce
1/4 cup water
2 - 3 pounds link sausage

Sauté onion, celery, and green pepper in salad oil. Add all remaining ingredients, except water and sausage. Simmer sauce for one hour. Refrigerate for 1 to 2 days. An hour or so before serving, simmer sausage in water, then brown. Cut sausages into two or three pieces, depending on size of links. Add sausage to heated sauce. Dish up individual servings or present in bowl with your favorite garnish. Great side dish with favorite egg recipe.

Submitted by Island Escape B&B, Gig Harbor Area

♥ ## Angel Hair Pasta With Eggs ♥

2 tablespoons sesame seed oil
2 cups angel hair pasta, cooked
1 1/2 cups diced fresh tomatoes
1/2 cup finely chopped green onions
1/2 cup diced green chilies
Salt & pepper, to taste
4 eggs, lightly beaten
1/2 cup half and half
1/2 cup mozzarella cheese, grated
1/2 cup Gruyère cheese, grated

Lightly brown cooked pasta in sesame seed oil for 5 to 7 minutes. Add tomatoes, onions, chilies, salt, and pepper. Toss lightly and cook until onions are tender (5 minutes). Blend eggs and half and half. Pour over pasta. Cover and cook until set, about 12 minutes. Remove from heat. Mix cheeses and sprinkle over eggs. Slide onto platter when ready to serve. Cut into small wedges.

Submitted by Run of the River, Leavenworth

♥ ## Rice Casserole ♥

1/2 stick butter
1/4 small onion, chopped
1 cup slivered almonds
1 can sliced mushrooms
2 cans beef consommé
1/2 pound shredded cheddar cheese
1 3/4 cups minute rice

Sauté onion in butter. Toast almonds and add to onions. Mix in mushrooms, consommé, cheese, and rice. Bake in covered casserole dish at 325° for 1 1/4 hours. This recipe can also be cooked in the microwave on high for 30 to 35 minutes. Makes 12 - 1/2 cup servings, as a side dish for eggs.

Submitted by Katy's Inn, La Conner

♥ **Foxy Fries** ♥

1 small potato, peeled
& sliced 1/4" thick

Molly McButter Sour
Cream Sprinkles®, to
taste

Peel potato, and slice with serrated knife into pieces about 1/4" thick. Spray frying pan with Pam® nonstick cooking spray. Spread potatoes in single layer in pan. Sprinkle with Molly McButter®. Cook on medium heat until done and lightly browned.

Submitted by Foxbridge B&B, Poulsbo

♥ **Jones Dairy Farm National Finalist Innkeepers Lumber Baron Potatoes** ♥

5 cups partially pre-
cooked (half-way)
potatoes, quartered &
sliced 1/4" thick
2 cups chopped onion
Butter or margarine
2 teaspoons garlic salt
1/2 teaspoon black
pepper
1/2 teaspoon thyme

2 tablespoons dry
parsley flakes
1/2 teaspoon sage
1/2 teaspoon rosemary
18 ounces Jones®
bulk sausage
8 ounces shredded Swiss,
Monterey jack, or
cheddar cheese

Brown potatoes in hot buttered skillet. Spread evenly in ungreased 9" x 13" pan or casserole dish. Sauté onions in butter until translucent. Distribute evenly over potatoes. Combine spices and sprinkle over potato/onion mixture. Using same skillet crumble and cook sausage, drain well, and stir into potatoes. Sprinkle cheese on top and bake uncovered at 350° for 30 minutes. Cut into squares and serve with your favorite eggs or as a side dish for dinner. This is a great "do ahead" dish for busy innkeepers. It can be refrigerated before cheese is added. Add extra baking time. Dish also holds well, foil-covered, at 200°.

Submitted by 1908 Cooney Mansion, Aberdeen (Cosmopolis)

♥ # Potato-Apple-Sausage Supreme ♥

4 - 6 ounces bulk
  chorizo sausage
1 tablespoon butter
3 large potatoes, thinly
  sliced
1 small red onion,
  thinly sliced
2 apples, Granny Smith
  or Golden Delicious,
  sliced

8 eggs
1 tablespoon water
2 tablespoons chopped,
  fresh parsley
Salt & pepper,
  to taste
Romano cheese,
  to taste

Sauté chorizo sausage thoroughly, retaining any drippings. Remove sausage from skillet. Add butter to skillet and cook potatoes and onions until tender (about 15 minutes). Add sliced apples, stir gently, and cook for 5 minutes. Blend eggs, water, parsley, salt, and pepper with whisk. Return chorizo to skillet(s), toss, cover with egg mixture, and cook until set, about 15 minutes. Just before serving sprinkle with grated Romano cheese. Slide onto a platter, cut into wedges, and serve immediately. Makes 8 - 12 servings. Use 2 nonstick skillets and serve on individual platters. Recipe is easily cut in half to serve a smaller group.

Submitted by Run of the River, Leavenworth

www.wbbg.com

♥ ## Southern Hashbrowns ♥

1 pkg. Southern hashbrown potatoes	1 can cream of mushroom soup
1 (8-ounce) carton sour cream	2 cups crushed Corn Flakes® cereal
1 stick melted butter	1/2 cup melted butter
2 cups shredded cheese	

Mix potatoes, sour cream, 1 stick melted butter, shredded cheese, and soup together in casserole and refrigerate overnight. In the morning, mix Corn Flakes® and 1/2 cup melted butter. Put on top of casserole. Bake at 350° for 50 minutes.

Submitted by Angeles Inn, Port Angeles

♥ ## Parmesan Tomatoes ♥

4 Roma tomatoes, cut in half	Garlic salt, to taste
Butter	Grated Parmesan cheese
	Parsley, to taste

Cut tomatoes in half. Butter top of each tomato half. Sprinkle with garlic salt and then cheese. Dust top with parsley. Broil for 5 to 8 minutes or until cheese is melted. Makes 4 servings.

Submitted by DeVoe Mansion, Tacoma

♥ ## Stuffed Walla Walla Sweets ♥

4 medium Walla Walla
  sweet onions, peeled
2/3 pound bulk pork
  sausage
3/4 cup bread crumbs
1/3 cup grated cheddar
  cheese
1 egg, lightly beaten
3 tablespoons milk

2 tablespoons chopped
  Italian parsley
1/4 teaspoon ground
  cinnamon
1/2 teaspoon sugar
Salt & freshly ground
  pepper, to taste
1 slice bacon, cut into
  4 pieces (opt.)

Peel onions and cut 1/2" off the top and bottom of each. Bring large pan of water to boil; add onions and boil for 7 minutes. Drain onions and cool slightly. Remove centers from onions, leaving a shell of at least 3 layers. Reserve onion centers for stuffing. If you cannot easily push out an onion center, use a spoon to scoop out some of the flesh until the center comes free, or cut out the center with a knife. Set onion shells in lightly greased baking dish. Preheat oven to 350°. Fry sausage in skillet over medium heat until no pink remains, breaking it into small pieces as it cooks. Drain well; discard fat. Finely chop onion centers to make 2 cups. Combine onion, sausage, bread crumbs, cheese, egg, milk, parsley, cinnamon, and sugar with a pinch each of salt and pepper. Mix well and stuff mixture into onion shells. Top each with a piece of bacon, if desired, and bake until stuffing is very hot and onion is tender, for 30 to 40 minutes. Makes 4 servings.

Submitted by Green Gables Inn, Walla Walla

www.wbbg.com

♥ # Apple Chutney ♥

4 Golden Delicious apples, peeled, cored & cut into 1" chunks	1 cup apple vinegar 1/2 cup brown sugar 1/2 cup raisins

Combine all the ingredients in a saucepan. Cook over low heat for 2 hours, stirring occasionally. Allow 1 tablespoon for each person. Serve at room temperature. Makes 12 servings. This is great to accompany an egg dish for breakfast. Just plan on everyone disappearing when you prepare the dish - the fragrance of vinegar cooking! The flavor improves if refrigerated for 3 to 4 days before serving.

Submitted by All Seasons River Inn, Leavenworth

♥ # Hollandaise Sauce ♥

2 egg yolks 1/4 cup cream 4 tablespoons melted butter 1/8 teaspoon dry mustard	1/8 teaspoon salt 1 teaspoon fresh lemon juice Dash of cayenne pepper

Place all ingredients in microwave-safe bowl. Heat on high for 1 minute. Remove and whisk briskly. Heat on high for 1 minute more and whisk again. Heat at 80% power for 45 seconds. Remove and whisk. Continue heating at 80% power for 30 second intervals until sauce thickens to your liking. Note: Can be reheated at 40% power for 1 minute and whisked. Makes 3/4 cup sauce.

Submitted by Foxbridge B&B, Poulsbo

♥   **Baked Oatmeal**   ♥

2/3 cup granulated sugar	3 cups quick or old-
1/2 cup oil	fashioned oats
2 eggs, beaten	2 teaspoons baking
1 teaspoon salt	powder

Mix sugar, oil, and eggs until well blended. Add remaining ingredients and mix well. Pour into baking dish and bake at 350° for 30 to 35 minutes. Makes 6 - 8 servings. Variations: May add nuts, bananas, almonds, blueberries, raisins, or apples.

Submitted by Water's Edge B&B, Gig Harbor

♥   **Baked Oatmeal Served**   ♥
At Schnauzer Crossing

4 cups nonfat milk	2 cups old-fashioned
1 tablespoon margarine	oats
1/2 teaspoon salt	2 cups chopped Granny
1 1/2 tablespoons	Smith apples
cinnamon	1 cup raisins
1/2 cup brown sugar	1 cup chopped walnuts

Preheat oven to 350°. In large heavy pan bring milk, margarine, salt, cinnamon and brown sugar to a boil. Add remaining ingredients. Pour into baking pan and bake uncovered for 35 minutes. Makes 6 - 8 servings. Serve immediately with "snowballs": Roll lowfat vanilla ice cream balls in coconut. Freeze in mini muffin pans. Great fun!

Submitted by Schnauzer Crossing, Bellingham

♥ Fotheringham House Baked Oatmeal ♥

1 cup milk	2 cups rolled oats
2 eggs	1 1/2 teaspoons baking
1/4 cup oil	powder
1/2 cup brown	1 teaspoon cinnamon
sugar	1/2 teaspoon salt

Place first four ingredients in blender. Blend. Place remaining ingredients in a bowl. Combine the moist ingredients with dry and let stand for 5 minutes. Stir and pour into a buttered baking dish. Bake at 325° for 45 minutes. Serve hot, covered with applesauce and a little milk. Variations: Add 1/4 cup chopped nuts, dried cranberries, raisins, currants or dates to mixture before baking.

Submitted by The Fotheringham House, Spokane

♥ Illahee Manor Hot Italian Rice Cereal ♥

3 cups water	1 cup Italian Arborio
2 cups milk	rice (do not rinse)
1 cinnamon stick	1/2 cup raisins
3 tablespoons	1/2 cup sugar
butter	1 tablespoon vanilla

In saucepan over low heat, combine water, milk and cinnamon. Bring to a boil and keep at a very low simmer. In heavy saucepan over low heat, melt the butter. Add the rice and stir until well coated with butter, for about 1 minute. Stir in 1 1/2 cups of simmering milk mixture and the raisins into the rice. Simmer, stirring occasionally, until almost all the liquid is absorbed, for about 7 minutes. Add 1/2 cup of simmering milk mixture and continue to simmer, stirring occasionally, until almost all the liquid is absorbed, for about 5 minutes. Stir in another 1/2 cup of milk mixture and transfer the cinnamon stick from the milk pan to the rice pan. Continue adding the milk mixture 1/2 cup at a time, until the rice is just tender and creamily sauced, for about 45 minutes total cooking time. Add sugar and vanilla. Discard the cinnamon stick. Spoon into warm bowls and serve immediately. Sugar and butter can be served with rice. Makes 4 servings.

Submitted by Illahee Manor B&B, Bremerton

♥ **Island Escape's House Granola** ♥

4 cups rolled oats (I buy
  bulk from Natural
  Food Store)
1/4 cup unrefined
  safflower oil
1/4 cup honey
1 1/2 teaspoons vanilla

1/2 cup sesame
  seeds
1/2 cup chopped
  almonds, unsalted
1/2 cup chopped
  cashews, unsalted
1 cup raisins

Preheat oven to 350°. Toast rolled oats in oven for 15 minutes on a large shallow baking pan. (I use my largest cookie sheet.) Combine oil, honey and vanilla and heat on stove until warm. Mix seeds and nuts together in a large bowl. Mix liquid mixture with nuts, then add combined mixture to toasted oats. Blend well. Bake for 20 minutes, turning oats about every five minutes. (I set the timer to insure a nice uniform golden brown granola.) Add raisins when done cooking. (Coconut and dried unsweetened pineapple give a distinctive "island" touch.) Change this granola by adding your choice of dried fruits, i.e. apricots, apples, banana chips, cranberries, etc. We serve this House Granola with our Bowl of Hot Montana Whole Wheat Cereal. It is the main entree and is presented with juice, coffee or tea, in season fresh fruit plate and homemade muffins or a quick bread. (Credit for this recipe goes to Kim, my husband's daughter. She was a blue ribbon graduate of Peter Kump's New York Cooking School and she is currently a Pastry Chef in Sante Fe, New Mexico. Several of Kim's recipes are incorporated in our menus at Island Escape B&B.)

Submitted by Island Escape B&B, Gig Harbor Area

♥ **Mom's Granola** ♥

4 cups old-fashioned
  oats
1 cup coconut flakes
1/2 cup wheat germ
1/4 cup toasted sesame
  seeds

1/4 cup raw sunflower
  seeds
1 cup slivered almonds
1/2 cup honey
1/2 cup olive oil
1 cup raisins

Mix together oats, coconut flakes, wheat germ, sesame seeds, sunflower seeds, and almonds. Combine honey and oil in small saucepan and bring to a boil. Stir honey-oil into dry ingredients until all ingredients are moist. Spread onto 2 cookie sheets and bake at 300° for 30 minutes. Cool; then add raisins and store in airtight containers.

Submitted by Katy's Inn, La Conner

♥ Otters Pond Oatmeal Pudding ♥

2 1/4 cups quick cooking oatmeal or old-fashioned oatmeal, uncooked
3/4 cup firmly packed brown sugar
3/4 cup raisins or dried cranberries
1 teaspoon ground cinnamon
1/2 teaspoon salt (opt.)
3 1/3 cups skim milk
4 egg whites, lightly beaten or 1/2 cup egg substitute
1 tablespoon vegetable oil
1 tablespoon vanilla
Vanilla yogurt and thinned seedless blackberry jam

Preheat oven to 350°. Spray an 8" square baking dish with nonstick cooking spray. In a large bowl combine oatmeal, brown sugar, raisins or dried cranberries, cinnamon and salt; mix well. In a medium bowl combine milk, egg whites, oil and vanilla; mix well. Add to dry ingredients, mixing well. Pour into the prepared baking dish. Bake for 55 to 60 minutes or until center is set and firm to the touch. Cool slightly. Serve with vanilla yogurt and thinned fruit jam, if desired. Store leftover pudding tightly covered in refrigerator or freezer. (Cut into serving pieces if freezing.) Note: To reheat, place single serving in microwave-safe bowl. Cook on high (100% power) for about 30 seconds or until warm.

Submitted by Otters Pond B&B of Orcas Island, Orcas Island

♥ Overnight Apple Oatmeal ♥

2 cups milk
1/4 cup brown sugar
1 tablespoon melted butter
1/4 teaspoon salt
1/2 teaspoon cinnamon
1 cup rolled oats
1 cup chopped apple
1/2 cup raisins
1/2 cup chopped walnuts

Grease the inside surface of a crock pot. Measure into it milk, brown sugar, melted butter, salt and cinnamon. Stir to combine with a wire whisk. Add oats, apple, raisins and nuts. Mix well and cover pot. Just before going to bed, turn on the crock pot at low speed. The cereal will be ready for morning. Serve with milk. Makes 4 servings.

Submitted by Trumpeter Inn B&B, San Juan Island

♥ # Whole Grain Cereal ♥

2 1/2 cups water
1/3 cup brown rice
1/3 cup wheat berries
1/3 cup barley

2 tablespoons flax
  seed
1/2 cup golden raisins
1/2 cup raisins

Bring water to a boil and add the 1 cup plus 2 tablespoons of mixed grains. Cover and simmer for 25 minutes. After 25 minutes, add the golden raisins and raisins and continue to simmer, covered, for 15 minutes more. Serve. Makes 5 servings. If cooked ahead, transfer to microwave-safe dishes, cover and refrigerate until needed. To serve, microwave single servings on high for 1 to 2 minutes. May be served with fresh fruit, lowfat milk or brown sugar. Note: The mixture of grains may be varied according to personal taste. Vegan, if served with soy or rice milk.

Submitted by Kangaroo House B&B on Orcas Island,
Eastsound / Orcas Island

♥ # Windsong's Apple Oat Cereal ♥

6 tablespoons organic
  rolled oats
5 tablespoons apple
  cider
2 tablespoons dark
  brown sugar

2 tablespoons lemon juice
2 tablespoons heavy
  cream
1 medium Granny Smith
  apple, grated
Fresh berries for garnish

Soak oats in apple cider at least 8 hours or overnight. Dissolve brown sugar in lemon juice; add oat mixture. Add heavy cream and grated apple. Refrigerate. Garnish with fresh berries to serve.

Submitted by WindSong Inn, Orcas Island, San Juan Islands

House Specialties

Melissa Pigg ©

Napkin Folding

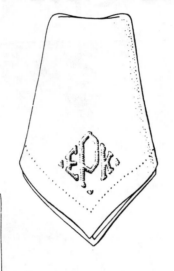

3

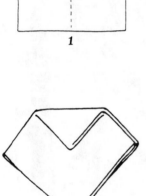

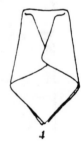

1

2

4

Elegance

1. Fold the napkin in quarters.
2. Place the napkin as shown with the free points at the bottom and the monogram or design, face down. Fold down the top points.
3. Fold the left point just past the center.
4. Repeat with right point and turn napkin over.

♥ Asparagus Crudìtes With Mayonnaise Verte ♥

1 1/2 pounds asparagus, with thin stalks, trimmed	2 tablespoons extra-virgin olive oil
Boiling water	1 tablespoon fresh lemon juice
Ice water	1 teaspoon Dijon mustard
1/2 cup packed fresh tarragon leaves	1/2 cup mayonnaise
	Salt & pepper, to taste

In large saucepan of boiling water, blanch asparagus for 1 minute. Transfer immediately to large bowl of ice water to stop cooking action. Drain and pat dry. In blender puree tarragon leaves with oil, lemon juice, and mustard until smooth. Stir puree into mayonnaise, and season with salt and pepper. Serve as a dip with asparagus. Makes 4 servings.

Submitted by Palisades B&B at Dash Point, Seattle / Tacoma

♥ Frosted Nuts ♥

1 cup sugar	1 teaspoon pure vanilla
6 tablespoons evaporated milk	3 1/2 cups whole pecans or walnuts

Mix together sugar and milk. Cook over medium low heat. Let boil until it comes to a soft ball stage, stirring to keep it from scorching. When done, stir in vanilla and nuts. Stir and pour out on waxed paper to cool. Store in air tight containers until ready to serve. These are really good.

Submitted by The Shepherd's Inn B&B, Salkum

♥ ## Sausage And Cheese Balls ♥

1/2 cup Bisquick® mix
1/2 pound cooked &
   drained sausage
1/4 cup milk

1/2 cup shredded
   cheddar cheese
1/4 teaspoon cayenne
   pepper

Mix all ingredients together and roll into small balls. Place on cookie sheet. Bake at 350° for 10 to 12 minutes or until lightly browned. Makes 12 sausage balls. You can make ahead and freeze.

Submitted by Nantucket Inn, Anacortes

♥ ## Devonshire Cream ♥

1 cup heavy cream,
   whipped to soft
   peaks

1/3 cup sour cream
1 tablespoon
   confectioners sugar

Whip heavy cream to soft peaks. Add sour cream and confectioners sugar. Whip until stiff - don't turn into butter! Serve immediately. Will not hold more than a few hours in refrigerator. Use with lemon curd as accompaniment with scones, huckleberry or blueberry pancakes, sauces and tarts.

Submitted by The Fotheringham House, Spokane

♥ ## Homemade Devonshire Cream ♥

1/2 cup heavy whipping
   cream
1 tablespoon powdered
   sugar

3/4 cup cultured
   sour cream

Whip heavy whipping cream with the powdered sugar until soft peaks form. Add sour cream and beat until just fluffy and well combined. Place in a covered container and refrigerate until serving. Makes 1 1/2 cups cream.

Submitted by The Whalebone House,
Ocean Park - Long Beach Peninsula

♥   **Lemon Curd**   ♥

1/2 cup unsalted butter   **2 cups sugar**
Juice of 4 large lemons   **5 beaten eggs**
Grated rind of 1 lemon

In top of double boiler, combine butter, lemon juice, lemon rind and sugar. Heat until butter melts and add beaten eggs gradually. Cook, stirring constantly, until it thickens. Keep covered in refrigerator. Use with Devonshire cream as accompaniment with scones, huckleberry or blueberry pancakes, sauces and tarts.

Submitted by The Fotheringham House, Spokane

♥   **Orange Cream Cheese Spread**   ♥

16 ounces cream cheese,   **2 tablespoons orange**
   softened   **juice concentrate,**
1/2 cup powdered sugar   **thawed**
2 tablespoons grated   **2 tablespoons Cointreau**
   orange peel   **or orange liqueur (opt.)**

Combine cream cheese, powdered sugar, orange peel, juice concentrate, and liqueur thoroughly, by hand or in food processor. Cover and chill overnight.

Submitted by Channel House, Anacortes

♥ **Strawberry Rhubarb Freezer Jam** ♥

6 cups chopped
  rhubarb
3 cups sugar

1 (3-ounce) box
  strawberry Jello®
  (sugar-free is fine)

Mix together rhubarb and sugar and let stand overnight. The next day bring mixture to a boil and simmer for 10 to 12 minutes. Remove from heat and stir in Jello®. Let set until cold and freeze in small cartons. Makes 1 - 2 pints and will keep in the refrigerator for 1 to 2 weeks. This is quite easy to prepare and a favorite with the guest! We serve it with our fresh baked croissants, but it's great on hot biscuits or waffles.

Submitted by The Shepherd's Inn B&B, Salkum

♥ **Aland Pancake** ♥

4 cups milk
1 cup rice
2 eggs
1/2 cup sugar

3/4 cup wheat
  flour
1/2 teaspoon salt
Touch of cardamom

Cook milk and rice into a "porridge." Beat eggs together with sugar and add to rice mixture. Then stir in flour, salt and cardamom, plus more milk if the mixture is too thick. Pour mixture into a greased round baking pan or oven proof dish. Bake at 350° for approximately 35 to 40 minutes or until set. This is traditionally cut into wedges and served at room temperature with a topping of "prune soup" and whipped cream. Any fruit sauce may be used in place of prune soup. Makes 4 - 6 servings.

Submitted by Killarney Cove B&B, Federal Way

♥ Baked Cheese Blintz With Berry Topping ♥

Filling:
16 ounces cream cheese, softened
22 ounces ricotta cheese
3 egg yolks
1 1/2 tablespoons granulated sugar
1 1/2 teaspoons vanilla extract

Blintz:
3/4 cup butter, softened
1/3 cup sugar
8 eggs
1 cup all purpose flour
1 tablespoon baking powder
2 1/4 cups plain yogurt
3/4 cup orange juice

Berry Topping:
1 cup granulated sugar
3 tablespoons cornstarch
2 cups orange juice
1/4 cup lemon juice
1/4 cup butter
1 cup frozen blueberries or fresh strawberries

For Filling: In small bowl beat cream cheese until smooth. Add ricotta cheese, egg yolks, sugar, and vanilla. Mix thoroughly and set aside. For Blintz: In large bowl cream butter and sugar. Add eggs and beat well. In 2 separate bowls combine flour with baking powder, and yogurt with orange juice. Add alternately to egg mixture and stir until thoroughly blended. For Topping: Mix sugar and cornstarch in bowl. Add orange juice, lemon juice, and butter. Bring to rolling boil on stove and cook for 1 minute, stirring constantly. Add berries and let simmer for at least 5 minutes. Pour half of blintz batter into 9" x 13" greased glass baking dish. Cover with filling and spread evenly. Cover with remaining blintz batter. Bake at 350° for 50 minutes until golden brown. Microwave for 5 minutes if outside browns before center is set. Serve with Berry Topping. Can be refrigerated overnight before baking. Makes 14 servings.

Submitted by Hillside House B&B, San Juan Island

♥   # Croissant Sandwiches   ♥

2 croissants (Costco®)
Dijon mustard, to
  taste

2 slices Havarti cheese
2 slices Black Forest® or
  maple ham

Slice baked croissants in half. Spread bottom half with a thin layer of mustard. Fold cheese and ham into croissant and put top half back on. Bake on ungreased cookie sheet at 300° for about 5 minutes until cheese melts. Serve on plate with sliced fruit as side dish. Makes 2 sandwiches (2 servings). We serve this for our "Country Continental" treat.

Submitted by White Swan Guest House, La Conner (Mt. Vernon)

♥   # Croissant Soufflé   ♥

6 large croissants,
  chopped
8 ounces cream cheese,
  softened
1/2 cup butter, softened

3/4 cup maple syrup,
  divided
10 eggs
3 cups half and half
Cinnamon-sugar mixture

Butter Rum Sauce:
1 cup maple syrup
1/2 cup butter

1/4 cup rum
1 egg

Place croissants in well-buttered 9" x 13" glass pan. Mix cream cheese, 1/2 cup butter and 1/4 cup maple syrup until smooth. Spread on top of croissants, leaving some openings through which to pour egg mixture. Beat eggs, half and half and 1/2 cup maple syrup. Pour over croissants and sprinkle with cinnamon-sugar. Cover and refrigerate overnight. Uncover and bake at 350° for 50 to 55 minutes. Serve with Butter Rum Sauce: Heat maple syrup and butter until melted. Add rum. Beat egg and whisk in 1/2 cup of syrup/butter mixture. Add back to syrup pan and heat and whisk until it reaches 180°. Makes 8 servings.

Submitted by Autumn Pond B&B, Leavenworth

♥ Glazed Pear & Golden Raisin-Filled Crepes ♥ With Custard Sauce

2 firm, ripe Bosc pears
1 1/2 tablespoons butter
1/4 cup golden raisins
1 1/2 tablespoons sugar
4 prepared crepes

Custard Sauce:
1/2 cup half and half
1 large egg yolk
1 tablespoon sugar
Pinch of salt

Preheat oven to 350°. Cut peeled pears into eighths and trim core. In heavy 8" skillet heat butter over moderately high heat until foamy. Add pear wedges and raisins, sauté for 1 minute. Sprinkle with sugar and cook until sugar is caramelized and pears are tender, 2 to 4 minutes. Fill crepes with fruit, roll up, and place in buttered baking dish. For Custard Sauce: In small saucepan heat half and half over moderate heat until it barely simmers. In small bowl whisk egg yolk and sugar with salt. Whisk 1/4 cup of half and half into yolk mixture, then pour into remaining half and half. Cook sauce until slightly thickened, about 3 minutes (do not boil!) Chill for 30 minutes. Heat crepes for approximately 15 minutes at 350° and serve with sauce.

Submitted by Palisades B&B at Dash Point, Seattle / Tacoma

♥ Heavenly Crab-Filled Croissants ♥

4 large croissants
8 eggs
3 tablespoons milk
1 tablespoon parsley, minced
1/3 cup mushrooms, chopped

1/2 cup fresh crab, chopped
4 tablespoons butter
1/4 cup Swiss cheese, shredded
1/4 cup cheddar cheese, shredded

Warm croissants in oven 5 minutes before filling. In bowl beat eggs and milk together. Add parsley, mushrooms, and crab. Melt butter in skillet. Pour egg mixture into skillet, cooking and stirring over low heat until creamy. Preheat broiler. Slice croissants, leaving attached. Fill bottom half with egg mixture and sprinkle both sides with cheese. Broil open-face until cheese melts.

Submitted by Albatross B&B, Anacortes

♥ ## Island Crab Delight ♥

1/2 cup fresh crab meat
1 cup cheddar cheese,
   grated
4 green onions,
   chopped
4 hard-boiled eggs,
   sliced & mashed

1/2 cup mayonnaise (I
   use Hain's® eggless)
10 - 12 Spanish olives,
   stuffed with pimento
Whole wheat English
   muffins
Salt, to taste

Put peeled, hard-boiled eggs in egg slicer and then mash with a fork. Mix together crab meat, cheese, onions, mashed eggs, mayonnaise and olives. Put in refrigerator overnight. Next morning: Lightly butter muffin halves. Spread with crab mixture and lightly salt. Broil for 4 to 7 minutes until lightly browned. Cut into halves. Present on plate with curly endive leaf and favorite in season fresh fruit slices.

Submitted by Island Escape B&B, Gig Harbor Area

♥ ## La Cachette Surprise ♥

3 - 4 eggs, beaten
1/4 - 1/2 cup heavy cream
   or whipping cream
Sliced, plain white bread,
   to taste
Soft, plain lowfat or
   regular cream cheese,
   to taste, cut in chunks

Variety of fruit, cooked
   meats, vegetables, jams,
   preserves, etc. (opt.)
Shredded cheese, any
   variety, to taste
Powdered sugar (opt.)
Variety of syrups (opt.)

Beat eggs and cream together in a bowl. Tear up slices of white bread into bite-sized pieces. Place in a baking dish that has been sprayed with Pam®. Place chunks of cream cheese over the top of the bread pieces. Now the creativity begins. You can put any cut up fruit sausage, bacon, vegetables, jams, preserves or anything else you can think of (or all of these) on top of the cream cheese. If you leave the meat out, this is a wonderful dish for vegetarians who eat cheese and eggs. Pour egg mixture over the other ingredients. Sprinkle shredded cheese over the top. Bake at 350° for 20 to 30 minutes (until the egg is cooked). Cut into squares (or triangles, rectangles, whatever you prefer) and serve with a sprinkling of powdered sugar. This can also be served with a variety of syrups (raspberry, boysenberry, maple, orange, etc.). This is the simplest, most creative breakfast you'll ever make! It can be made the night before and placed in the refrigerator. This is an especially good recipe since you can make use of whatever is in season at the time you prepare it. We've even put smoked salmon in ours.

Submitted by La Cachette B&B, Seabeck

♥ ## Mediterranean Vegetable Pie ♥

1 large onion,
  sliced
Olive oil, to sauté
1/3 cup water
3 medium zucchini,
  sliced into 1/2" pieces
2 yellow squash,
  sliced into 1/2" pieces
1 small can button
  mushrooms, drained

1 can Roma tomatoes,
  drained & sliced
Salt, pepper, garlic and
  Italian herbs, to taste
3 eggs
1/2 - 3/4 cup whipping
  cream
Parmesan cheese, to taste
Walnuts or pine nuts
Unbaked pie shell

Sauté onions in olive oil for 5 minutes over medium heat. Add water, cover and cook for 3 minutes. Add zucchini and yellow squash. Cover and cook for 2 minutes. Remove lid, let liquid cook off. Combine with drained mushrooms and tomatoes. Add salt, pepper, garlic and Italian herbs, to taste. In blender combine eggs and whipping cream. (Don't beat, just blend together.) Put unbaked pie shell in pie plate. Sprinkle with Parmesan cheese, to taste. Add drained vegetables. Sprinkle with more Parmesan cheese. Slowly pour egg mixture over pan. Sprinkle with walnuts or pine nuts. Bake at 350° for 40 minutes.

Submitted by Selah Inn, Belfair

Hints On Preparing Vegetables:

Vegetables are of great importance in everyone's daily diet. Working vegetables into the breakfast meal gives you a head start on our need for 3 - 5 servings daily.

- *Wait to wash vegetables until just before you are ready to use them.*
- *Prepare your vegetables as close as you can to the cooking time.*
- *Most vegetables with thin skins can be washed and scrubbed good without peeling them.*
- *For vegetables that require peeling, try to take off a thin peel of only the outer skin.*
- *Onions and garlic should be stored in dry air.*
- *Plastic bags will keep vegetables like green beans and celery fresher much longer.*

♥ ## Pennsylvania Dutch Potato Stuffing ♥

6 large potatoes,
  scrubbed, cubed into 1"
  pieces with skin left on
1 - 2 cups milk
Salt & pepper,
  to taste
1/2 cup butter

1 medium onion, chopped
3/4 cup chopped celery
2 cups soft bread cubes
  (leftover English
  muffins and other
  breakfast breads are
  great!)

Cube potatoes, cover with water and bring to a boil. Cook just until potatoes slip off a fork when pierced. Drain and mash potatoes, adding milk, salt and pepper. Set aside. In skillet, melt butter, then add chopped onion and celery and sauté for 3 minutes. Add bread cubes and continue to sauté until onions are limp and bread is slightly browned. Mix this mixture into mashed potatoes. Turn into buttered casserole dish. Can be refrigerated for up to 24 hours. Bake at 350° for 30 minutes. Makes 6 servings.

Submitted by Moon & Sixpence, San Juan Island

♥ ## Polenta ♥

1 1/2 sticks butter,
  softened
2 cups powdered sugar
4 eggs

1 egg yolk
1 teaspoon vanilla
1 cup all purpose flour
1/2 cup yellow cornmeal

Preheat oven to 375°. Butter and flour 12 (3 1/2") tartlette tins or muffin tins. Using an electric hand beater, cream the butter and powdered sugar until very fluffy. Add eggs and continue to mix very well. Add vanilla. Sift flour and combine with cornmeal. Add to the butter mixture, and beat on medium speed for about 5 to 6 minutes. Fill the tins almost to the top. Bake for 15 minutes or until golden brown. Do not overbake. After removing from the oven, cool on a wire rack. Dust with powdered sugar before serving. Serve warm. Makes 1 dozen. These are GREAT - rave reviews!

Submitted by English Tudor View, Seattle

♥　　Portabello Breakfast Caps　　♥

1 medium red bell
pepper
2 medium portabello
mushrooms, about
5" in diameter
6 leaves fresh spinach,
washed
4 ounces Jones® all
natural roll sausage,
browned & drained

4 large eggs
1 dash Tabasco sauce
Salt & pepper, to taste
1 tablespoon fresh
chives, snipped
1 teaspoon butter
1/2 cup cheddar cheese,
shredded, divided
2 tablespoons Parmesan
cheese, grated

Preheat oven to 350°. Over a gas flame char the red bell pepper, then place in plastic food bag. Seal and allow to stand for about 10 minutes, then peel away charred skin. Cut open pepper; remove stem, ribs and seeds, reserving the flesh. If prepared in advance, refrigerate until needed. Remove stems and gills from the portabello mushrooms and reserve for other uses. Place prepared mushroom caps on baking sheet and roast in oven for approximately 20 minutes. Meanwhile, prepare the remaining ingredients. In separate pan, briefly steam spinach just to wilt, or microwave on High for approximately 1 minute. Set aside. Sauté Jones® sausage until brown. Drain, and set aside. In small bowl whisk together eggs, Tabasco sauce, salt, pepper and chives. In small nonstick skillet or omelet pan melt butter, then add egg mixture and scramble to moist scramble stage. Add browned sausage and 1/4 cup grated cheddar and combine just to melt cheese. Avoid letting eggs get too dry. ASSEMBLY: Line each mushroom cap with a layer of the wilted spinach leaves, then a layer of roasted red pepper. Divide the scrambled egg/sausage mixture evenly on top of the mushrooms. Sprinkle with remaining cheddar and Parmesan cheeses and return to oven long enough to melt cheese, for approximately 1 to 2 minutes. Makes 2 servings. With a serrated knife, slice each mushroom cap and offset slightly to display layers to good advantage. Garnish with fresh, vine-ripened tomato slices and fresh herbs.

Submitted by Kangaroo House B&B on Orcas Island,
Eastsound / Orcas Island

♥ Shrimp In A Cloud ♥

6 slices French bread,
  lightly toasted
1/2 cup mayonnaise
1/2 cup sour cream
2 teaspoons lemon juice
Dash of salt

Dash of cayenne pepper
1 pound small shrimp,
  cooked & cleaned
6 egg whites
2 cups shredded
  Havarti cheese

Toast bread lightly on both sides. Mix mayonnaise, sour cream, lemon juice, salt, and cayenne pepper. Fold in well-drained shrimp. Separately whip egg whites until stiff and fold in cheese. Spoon shrimp mixture onto bread. Top with spoonfuls of cheese mixture to cover shrimp. Bake at 400° for about 10 minutes until golden brown. Serve immediately. Makes 6 servings.

Submitted by Scandinavian Gardens Inn, Long Beach Peninsula

♥ Amaretto Bread Pudding ♥

1 - 1 1/2 pound loaf
  French bread, cubed
  or torn
1 quart half and half
1 1/2 cups brown sugar

3 eggs
1 tablespoon almond
  flavoring
1 cup almonds, sliced

Sauce:
1 egg
2 cups powdered sugar

1/2 pound butter
1/3 cup Amaretto liqueur

Pour half and half over bread cubes. Add brown sugar, eggs, almond flavoring and almonds. Mix well. Pour into buttered 9" x 11" pan. Bake at 350° for 40 minutes. For sauce: Mix egg and powdered sugar. Melt butter in saucepan. Add powdered sugar mixture. Cook until smooth. Take off heat and add Amaretto. Cut pudding into squares and serve hot with warm sauce and whipping cream. Makes 12 servings.

Submitted by 1908 Cooney Mansion, Aberdeen (Cosmopolis)

♥ **Bread Pudding With** ♥
Cran-Raspberry Topping

1/2 loaf (1 pound size) French bread, torn into 1" pieces	1/3 cup granulated sugar
	1/2 teaspoon ground cinnamon
2 tablespoons raisins or currants or dried cranberries	Dash of salt
	1 1/2 cups milk
3 eggs	2 tablespoons packed brown sugar

<u>Cran-Raspberry Topping</u>:	1 cup sugar
10 ounces frozen raspberries, thawed	1 cup cranberries, frozen or thawed

Grease square pan (9" x 9" x 2"). Spread bread evenly in pan. Sprinkle with raisins or currants or dried cranberries. Beat eggs, granulated sugar, cinnamon and salt in medium bowl. Stir in milk; pour over bread. Sprinkle with brown sugar. Cover tightly and refrigerate for at least 2 hours, but no longer than 24 hours. Heat oven to 325°. Bake uncovered for 50 to 60 minutes until golden brown. Serve with topping: Drain raspberries, reserving 1/2 cup juice. Mix juice and sugar in 2 quart saucepan. Heat to boiling; boil for 5 minutes. Stir in raspberries and cranberries; reduce heat. Simmer for about 3 minutes, stirring occasionally, until cranberries are tender, but do not burst. Makes 6 servings.

Submitted by The Churchyard Inn, Uniontown

♥ Breakfast Bread Pudding With Blueberries ♥

4 - 5 slices day-old white
    bread, crusts removed
3 - 4 ounces cream cheese
Cinnamon-sugar mixture
    (1 tablespoon sugar
    mixed with 1/4 teaspoon
    ground cinnamon)
1 cup fresh or thawed
    blueberries

1/4 cup brown sugar,
    divided
1 tablespoon butter,
    diced
4 eggs
1 cup milk
1 teaspoon vanilla
    extract

Preheat oven to 350°. Spread sliced bread with cream cheese and sprinkle with cinnamon-sugar. Cut bread into cubes and place in bottom of greased 8" square pan. Distribute berries over bread cubes. Sprinkle half the brown sugar and all of the butter over the bread. Beat together eggs, milk and vanilla and pour over cubes. Sprinkle with remaining brown sugar. Set pan in larger shallow pan; add 1" hot water after pan has been placed on oven rack. Bake for 35 to 40 minutes or until a knife inserted in center comes out clean. Cool pudding before cutting into squares. Can be served with cream or fresh berry sauce or plain. Makes 4 servings.

Submitted by Boreas B&B Inn, Long Beach

♥ Peach Bread Pudding ♥

1 (29-ounce) can
    peaches, drained
3/4 cup sugar
3 1/2 cups nonfat milk
6 large eggs

2 teaspoons vanilla
1/2 cup peach Schnapp's
10 cups cubed scones,
    popovers, or bread (or
    any assortment)

Spray 9" x 13" Pyrex® baking dish with nonstick cooking spray. Drain peaches. Place half of peaches in processor and process to liquid. Dice other half of peaches and set aside. Combine sugar, milk, and eggs, and beat until well blended. Add vanilla, processed peach liquid, and Schnapp's. In large mixing bowl toss bread cubes with diced peaches. Pour milk mixture over bread and peaches, mix well, and let stand for 20 to 30 minutes until most of liquid is absorbed. Pour into sprayed baking dish, spread evenly, and bake in preheated oven at 350° for 1 hour or until firm. Place baking pan in larger pan filled with water 2/3 up the side (bain marie).

Submitted by Tower House B&B, San Juan Island

♥ # WindSong Bread Pudding With
Clear Rum Sauce ♥

5 large eggs, beaten
1 cup sugar
2 cups whipping cream
1/2 cup butter,
  melted
Dash of cinnamon

1 tablespoon vanilla
  extract
1/4 cup craisins
1/4 cup raisins
4 bread slices, cubed or
  torn into 1" pieces

Clear Rum Sauce:
1 cup sugar
2 cups water
1 teaspoon cinnamon
1 tablespoon butter

1/2 teaspoon cornstarch
1/4 cup water
1 tablespoon dark rum

Preheat oven to 350°. Beat eggs. Add sugar and combine thoroughly. Add cream, rebeat; add butter, cinnamon and vanilla extract and mix thoroughly. Add craisins, raisins and bread. Mix, cover and refrigerate for 4 - 8+ hours. Cook in a 9" x 9" pan, covered with aluminum foil. Place this pan in a larger pan filled with hot water to 1/2" from the top. Bake for 35 minutes, uncover and bake for an additional 10 minutes to brown top. Serve with Clear Rum Sauce: Dissolve sugar in 2 cups water in a saucepan. Add cinnamon and butter. When butter is dissolved, add cornstarch which has been dissolved in the 1/4 cup of water. Continue heating until sauce clears. Remove from heat and add rum.

Submitted by WindSong Inn, Orcas Island, San Juan Islands

www.wbbg.com

♥ ## Chocolate Oatmeal Decadence ♥

1/2 cup margarine
2 ounces unsweetened
chocolate squares
1 cup water
1 cup sugar
1 cup brown sugar,
packed
1/2 cup chocolate
syrup
1/2 cup coffee liqueur
1 1/2 teaspoons vanilla
3 extra large eggs
1 cup quick oatmeal,
uncooked

1 1/2 cups flour
1 teaspoon baking soda
1/2 teaspoon salt
1/2 cup butter
1/4 cup whipping cream
1 cup brown sugar,
packed
3/4 cup chopped pecans
1 (16-ounce) jar fudge
topping
2 cups whipping cream
1/4 cup plus 1 tablespoon
powdered sugar
1/2 teaspoon vanilla

Melt 1/2 cup margarine with unsweetened chocolate squares. Cool slightly. Pour margarine-chocolate mixture into large mixing bowl. Add water, 1 cup sugar, 1 cup brown sugar, chocolate syrup, coffee liqueur, vanilla, eggs and oatmeal. Beat well. Then add flour, baking soda and salt. Beat well. Pour into 3 greased and floured 9" round cake pans. Bottoms should be lined with waxed paper. Bake at 350° for 20 to 30 minutes or until toothpick inserted comes out clean. Meanwhile, in medium saucepan bring butter, 1/4 cup whipping cream, 1 cup brown sugar and pecans to a boil. Cook for 2 to 3 minutes and pour evenly over baked cake (while still in pans), dividing equally among layers. Place layers under broiler for a couple of minutes until bubbly. Watch closely as this may burn easily. Cool cake completely in refrigerator. Carefully remove from pans. Warm fudge topping just until spreadable and divide equally. Spread over each layer. Beat 2 cups whipping cream until stiff peaks form. Add powdered sugar and vanilla. Assemble by layering cake and whipped cream into a tower of decadence, ending with whipped cream and garnishing with chocolate curls.

Submitted by Stratford Manor, Bellingham

♥ # Chocolate Sin Pudding Cake ♥

3/4 cup all purpose flour
3/4 cup granulated sugar
1 1/2 teaspoons baking powder
1/2 teaspoon baking soda
1/4 teaspoon salt
1/3 cup + 1/4 cup unsweetened cocoa

1/2 cup milk
3 tablespoons butter or margarine, melted
1 teaspoon vanilla extract
1/2 cup firmly packed brown sugar
1 3/4 cups boiling water
Whipped cream or vanilla ice cream (opt.)

Preheat oven to 350°. Grease 9" square baking dish. Combine flour, granulated sugar, baking powder, baking soda, salt and 1/3 cup cocoa in medium bowl. Combine milk, butter and vanilla in measuring cup; stir into dry ingredients just until blended. Spoon batter evenly into prepared dish. Combine brown sugar and remaining 1/4 cup cocoa in small bowl. Sprinkle evenly over batter. Pour boiling water over entire mixture; do not stir. Bake for 35 to 38 minutes, until toothpick inserted in center comes out clean. Cool for 10 minutes. Serve with whipped cream or vanilla ice cream, if desired. Makes 8 servings.

Submitted by 1908 Cooney Mansion, Aberdeen (Cosmopolis)

Options For Chocolate Substitutions:

- *1 square unsweetened chocolate = 3 tablespoons cocoa plus 3 tablespoons shortening*
- *1 ounce bitter chocolate = 4 tablespoons cocoa plus 2 tablespoons butter*
- *6 ounce package of semi-sweet pieces, melted = 2 squares unsweetened chocolate plus 2 tablespoons shortening and 1/2 cup sugar*

♥ Chocolate Zucchini Cake - The Best! ♥

2 1/2 cups flour
6 tablespoons unsweetened baking cocoa powder
1/2 teaspoon baking powder
1 teaspoon baking soda
3/4 teaspoon cinnamon
1/2 teaspoon cloves
1/2 cup margarine
1/2 cup oil
1 3/4 cups white sugar
2 eggs
1 teaspoon vanilla
1/2 cup sour milk
2 cups grated zucchini
1/2 cup chocolate chips, divided
1/2 cup chopped nuts, if desired (opt.)

Preheat oven to 325°. Stir together dry ingredients and set aside. In large bowl cream together margarine, oil and sugar with electric mixer. Add eggs, vanilla and sour milk (or 2 tablespoons vinegar in 1/2 cup milk and let set for 15 minutes). Continue beating until well mixed. Stir in dry ingredients a little at a time. Mix well. Stir in grated zucchini. (Note: If using frozen zucchini it takes about twice as much. I grate zucchini when plentiful and freeze in 2-cup amounts in sandwich bags. Lightly squeeze excess water from 2 thawed bags before adding to your mix. The water is great for house plants!) Stir in 1/4 cup chocolate chips and nuts, if desired. Spread batter in greased 9" x 13" pan. Bake for about 15 minutes, then sprinkle top with another 1/4 cup chocolate chips. Bake for another 40 to 45 minutes. Knife inserted into middle should come out clean.

Submitted by The FARMHOUSE, Whidbey Island - Langley

♥ Clouds At Sunrise ♥

6 egg whites
3/4 teaspoon cream of tartar
2 cups sugar
2 cups crushed soda crackers (about 45)
3/4 cup chopped nuts
2 teaspoons vanilla
2 cups whipping cream, whipped
1 (21-ounce) can cherry pie filling

Preheat oven to 350°. Beat egg whites until frothy. Add cream of tartar, then gradually add sugar. Beat until stiff. Fold in crackers, nuts, and vanilla. Spread in well-buttered 9" x 13" baking dish. Bake at 350° for 25 minutes. Cool on rack. Whip cream, spread over the top, and spoon pie filling over the cream. Chill several hours or overnight.

Submitted by The Churchyard Inn, Uniontown

♥ **Easy Flan** ♥

2 tablespoons powdered
  milk
2 cups milk
3 eggs

1 teaspoon vanilla
4 tablespoons honey
Dash of nutmeg

Beat powdered milk into whole milk. Add eggs and beat until smooth. Add vanilla and honey, and stir until honey dissolves. Pour into soufflé dish and sprinkle lightly with nutmeg. Bake at 325° for 1 hour or until knife inserted into center comes out clean. Makes 6 servings.

Submitted by Heaven's Edge B&B, Silverdale

♥ **Lemon Lush** ♥

4 tablespoons sugar
1 stick margarine,
  softened
1 cup flour
1/2 cup chopped nuts
8 ounces cream cheese,
  softened

1 cup powdered sugar
1 (12-ounce) container
  Cool Whip®, divided
2 (3-ounce) boxes instant
  lemon pudding
3 cups milk
Chopped nuts for garnish

For Crust: Cream sugar and margarine; beat in flour and add nuts. Press into a 9" x 13" pan. Bake at 350° for 10 to 12 minutes. Cool crust. Cream together cream cheese and powdered sugar. Blend well and add half of the Cool Whip®. Spread over cooled baked crust. Mix together instant pudding and milk. Beat at low speed for 2 minutes and spread over cream cheese mixture in pan. Top with remaining Cool Whip® and sprinkle lightly with chopped nuts. Refrigerate until ready to serve. This is a popular dessert and a real hit with lemon lovers, and fairly easy to make! Attention, Chocolate Lovers: For a lovely chocolate dessert, just substitute instant chocolate pudding for the lemon.

Submitted by The Shepherd's Inn B&B, Salkum

♥ ## Luscious Lemon Cake ♥

4 ounces soft
  margarine
6 ounces castor sugar
  (very fine sugar)
2 eggs

6 ounces self-rising
  flour, sifted
Grated rind of 1
  lemon
4 tablespoons milk

Lemon Syrup:
3 rounded tablespoons
  powdered sugar, sifted

3 tablespoons fresh
  lemon juice

Grease and line with waxed paper a 2 pound loaf tin. Set oven at 350°. Cream margarine and sugar. Add eggs, sifted flour, finely grated lemon rind, and milk. Mix well to a soft dropping consistency. Pour into tin. Smooth top. Bake for 40 to 45 minutes until firm. For Lemon Syrup: Mix sifted powdered sugar and lemon juice. While cake is still warm, pour over cake. Leave in tin until completely cool. Do not peek at cake while in oven, it will drop in the middle. Delicious with a pot of tea for an afternoon snack.

Submitted by Beachside B&B, Gig Harbor

♥ ## Mango Delight ♥

2 (3-ounce) packages
  lemon gelatin
1 3/4 cups boiling water

8 ounces cream cheese
2 cups chopped
  fresh mangoes

Dissolve gelatin in boiling water. Cool until thickened, but not firm. Blend cream cheese and mangoes together in blender or food processor until smooth. Mix mango mixture and gelatin together until well blended. Pour into a mold or an 8" square pan and chill until firm. Makes 6 servings. Enjoy!

Submitted by Heaven's Edge B&B, Silverdale

♥ ## Peach Cobbler ♥

1 cup Bisquick® mix	1 cup sliced peaches
1 cup sugar, divided	1/2 cup butter
1/2 cup milk	1 tablespoon cinnamon

Mix Bisquick®, 1/4 cup sugar and milk together and put in bottom of baking dish. Mix the rest of sugar into peaches and pour on top of Bisquick® mixture. Cube butter and place on top of peaches. Sprinkle cinnamon over all and place in oven at 350° for 1 hour or until lightly brown.

Submitted by Nantucket Inn, Anacortes

♥ ## Strawberry Pie ♥

Pastry shell:

1 cup all purpose flour	6 tablespoons butter
1 tablespoon sugar	1 egg yolk
	1 tablespoon ice water

Filling:

8 ounces cream cheese, softened	1 - 1 1/2 quarts strawberries, washed & hulled
3 tablespoons sour cream	Water, as needed
Granulated sugar, as needed for sprinkling	3 tablespoons cornstarch
	1 cup sugar
	Red food coloring

For pastry shell: Combine flour and sugar, then work in butter. Add egg yolk and ice water. Work until dough holds together (do not overwork). Pat into flat round, wrap and chill until firm. Roll out between sheets of waxed paper. Remove top paper and turn pastry into pan. Prick dough with fork. Bake at 375° for 15 to 20 minutes. Cool for 1 hour before filling. For pie filling: Beat cream cheese and sour cream until fluffy. Spread onto cooled pastry shell and sprinkle lightly with sugar. Refrigerate. Mash washed and hulled berries to make 1 cup. Add enough water to cornstarch to make a thick paste. Mix 1 cup sugar with cornstarch paste and 1 cup mashed berries. Cook over medium heat, stirring until blended. Boil for about 1 minute. Add a little red food coloring and cool. Fill pie shell with the remaining berries. Pour the syrup mixture over the top. Refrigerate for 1 hour.

Submitted by Samish Point by the Bay, La Conner (Mt. Vernon)

♥   # Syllabub   ♥

Juice and grated rind of
  1 lemon
1/2 cup sugar

1/2 cup sherry
2 cups heavy
  cream

Combine all of the ingredients and beat until stiff (for about 5 minutes with electric beater or 20 minutes with a whisk). Refrigerate for 30 minutes and serve. Makes 6 servings.

Submitted by Heaven's Edge B&B, Silverdale

♥   # Water Whip No Fail Pie Crust   ♥

1/4 cup water
1 tablespoon milk
3/4 cup shortening

1 teaspoon salt
2 cups flour
4 sheets waxed paper

Bring water and milk to a boil. Quickly pour over shortening and salt. Stir and whip until smooth. Add flour all at once and mix well. Divide dough into two balls. Roll out each ball between two sheets of waxed paper. To roll very thin, pick up papers, turn over, gently remove and put back wrinkled paper, and roll out dough again. When large enough to fit a 9" pie pan, remove one sheet of waxed paper, turn other sheet with dough upside down into pie pan. Gently peel paper off of pie crust. Place second ball between new waxed papers and repeat for top crust. Fill with your favorite fruit filling and bake.

Submitted by The Fotheringham House, Spokane

♥ WindSong Brûlée ♥

1 cup steel cut oats, cooked
1/2 cup wild rice, cooked
1/2 cup whipping cream
2 tablespoons dark brown sugar
2 large eggs
3 teaspoons granulated sugar, divided

Preheat oven to 425°. In pre-cooking the cereals, use heavy cream and water as directed when cooking the oats. Cook the rice in boiling water for 2 periods of 20 minutes. Mix together after draining and cooking. Lightly beat whipping cream. Add brown sugar and eggs and mix until eggs are fully incorporated into whipped cream. Lightly grease 6 (4-ounce) Pyrex® dishes with softened butter. Add 2 tablespoons of cereal (to fill half full). Cover cereal with custard mixture (cream, eggs and sugar mixture). Do not fill the dishes, leave 1/4"+ for the custard to rise. Place on baking pan and bake for 15 minutes. Remove from oven, sprinkle 1/2 teaspoon granulated sugar on top of each custard and caramelize either under broiler or with torch. Custard should be lightly browned, and set on top, but a little liquidy. Garnish with toasted chopped nuts or diced fresh fruit.

Submitted by WindSong Inn, Orcas Island, San Juan Islands

♥ Mom's Frangos ♥

1/2 pound butter
2 cups powdered sugar
4 squares baking chocolate, melted
3 eggs (or substitute)
2 teaspoons vanilla
1 teaspoon peppermint extract
Slivered or chopped almonds

In electric mixer or blender mix butter and powdered sugar well. Add melted baking chocolate. Beat in eggs, one at a time, vanilla, and peppermint extract. Sprinkle bottom of small waxed paper cups and/or demitasse cups with chopped or slivered almonds and frango mixture. Put more nuts on top. Freeze until ready to serve.

Submitted by The Fountains B&B, Gig Harbor

♥ **Peanut Butter Balls** ♥

1 can Eagle Brand®
  sweetened condensed
  milk
1/2 cup margarine,
  melted
1 pound powdered sugar

1 - 1 1/2 cups crunchy
  peanut butter, or to taste
12 ounces real chocolate
  chips
4 squares chocolate
  almond bark

Mix together sweetened condensed milk, melted margarine, powdered sugar and peanut butter until a soft, firm ball forms and it is easy to roll into small 3/4" balls. Chill mixture for 1 hour or more. When firm, form into balls. Chill again for 1/2 hour or so. Then dip in the following chocolate mixture: Melt chocolate chips, using about 1/4 package at a time, mixed with 1 square chocolate almond bark. Melt together in microwave in a small glass bowl for about 30 seconds at a time. Stir and melt for another 30 seconds until smooth and creamy. Dip balls with a fork one at a time. Let excess chocolate drip back into bowl and place on waxed paper to dry. If the balls are well-chilled, the chocolate hardens quickly and leaves a nice shiny surface. Place in small candy wrappers. These are especially fun and easy to make for the holidays.

Submitted by The Shepherd's Inn B&B, Salkum

♥ **Almond Roca Cookies** ♥

1 cup butter, softened
1/2 cup brown sugar
1/2 cup white sugar
1 teaspoon vanilla

1 egg yolk
1 cup flour
12 ounces chocolate chips
1/4 cup chopped almonds

Combine all ingredients except chocolate chips and almonds. Spread in 10" x 13" pan. Bake at 325° for 25 minutes. Remove from oven and sprinkle with chips. Bake for 3 minutes more and spread chocolate with spatula. Sprinkle top with almonds. Cut into squares while still warm. Chill in pan. Remove carefully.

Submitted by Trumpeter Inn B&B, San Juan Island

♥ California Lemon Sours ♥

Crust:
1 cup margarine
1/4 teaspoon salt

1 cup + 2 tablespoons flour

Filling:
3 eggs
1 1/2 cups brown sugar
1 cup coconut
3/4 cup chopped walnuts

1/4 teaspoon baking powder
3/4 teaspoon vanilla

Frosting:
2 cups powdered sugar
3 tablespoons lemon juice

3 tablespoons lemon rind

Mix crust ingredients to a fine crumb texture with a pastry blender. Spread in 9" x 12" pan. Bake at 350° for 10 minutes. For filling: Beat eggs, add remaining filling ingredients. Mix well. Spread on the crust when it is taken from oven. Bake at 350° for 20 minutes more. Mix frosting ingredients to creamy consistency. Spread onto cookie mixture while warm. Cool, cut into squares.

Submitted by 1908 Cooney Mansion, Aberdeen (Cosmopolis)

♥ Chelsea Station "4-6-20" Sugar Cookies ♥

1 pound butter, softened
1 1/2 cups sugar
5 cups flour

2 teaspoons vanilla or the juice of 1 lemon or other flavoring you like

Cream butter and sugar and add flour. Add flavoring. Scoop dough in 1/2 ounce balls onto ungreased cookie sheet and flatten with the bottom of a sugared glass. Hint: Place cookies at the back of the baking sheet. Bake at 350° for 7 to 10 minutes. May be frosted with 2/3 box powdered sugar and the juice and zest of a lemon, or Nutella® or any favorite frosting.

Submitted by Chelsea Station on the Park, Seattle

♥ **Eagles Nest Inn Chocolate Chip Cookies** ♥

3 1/2 cups flour, unsifted
1 teaspoon salt
1 teaspoon baking soda
2 sticks margarine
3/4 cup brown sugar, packed
3/4 cup granulated sugar
1 teaspoon vanilla
2 large eggs
12 ounces chocolate chips
3/4 - 1 cup chopped walnuts (opt.)

Preheat oven to 350°. In bowl combine flour, salt, and baking soda. Cream margarine, brown sugar, and granulated sugar. Add vanilla and eggs, and mix just until smooth. Add flour mixture and mix until blended. Batter will be stiff. Stir in chocolate chips and walnuts if used. Form balls about the size of a walnut. Place on ungreased cookie sheet. Bake for 12 minutes. Cool for several minutes before removing from cookie sheet to cool. Makes 5 dozen cookies. Since starting in 1989, the Eagles Nest Inn has served 117,770 chocolate chip cookies to guests.

Submitted by Eagles Nest Inn, Whidbey Island - Langley

♥ **English Toffee Bars** ♥

4 ounces butter
4 ounces brown sugar
1 egg yolk
2 ounces plain flour
2 ounces oatmeal

Topping:
3 ounces plain chocolate
1 ounce butter
Chopped nuts, to taste

Grease jelly roll tin. Set oven at 370°. Beat butter, sugar, and egg yolk. Add flour and oats. Press mixture into tin and bake for 15 to 20 minutes. Cool slightly. Melt plain chocolate and butter and spread over mixture in tin. Cover with chopped walnuts. Cut into bars while warm, but leave in tin until completely cold. Serve as an afternoon snack.

Submitted by Beachside B&B, Gig Harbor

♥ Lover's Retreat Chocolate Coconut Brownies ♥

3 ounces cream cheese
6 tablespoons butter or
    margarine, divided
3/4 cup sugar, divided
3 eggs, divided
1/2 cup + 1 tablespoon
    flour, divided
1 1/2 cups flaked coconut

1 cup sliced almonds,
    divided
6 ounces semisweet
    chocolate chips
1/2 teaspoon vanilla
1/2 teaspoon baking
    powder
Pinch of salt

For Top Layer: Beat cream cheese and 2 tablespoons butter until soft. Beat in 1/4 cup sugar. Stir in 1 egg, 1 tablespoon flour and all of the coconut. Fold in 1/2 cup sliced almonds. Set aside. For Bottom Layer: Melt chocolate chips and 4 tablespoons butter over low heat; (in saucepan or in microwave) watch carefully! Remove from heat. Stir in 1/2 cup sugar and vanilla. Beat in 2 eggs. Stir in 1/2 cup flour, baking powder and salt. Fold in 1/2 cup sliced almonds. Spread chocolate batter into an 8" square greased pan. Spread cream cheese batter on top. Bake at 350° (325° if using glass pan) for 35 to 40 minutes or until toothpick inserted into center comes out almost clean. Do not overbake! Can drizzle melted chocolate over brownies. Cool. Cut into squares. Makes 16 sinfully delicious brownies. Enjoy!

Submitted by The FARMHOUSE, Whidbey Island - Langley

www.wbbg.com

♥ # Mrs. King's Cookies ♥

2 cups butter,
  softened
2 cups brown sugar
2 cups white sugar
4 eggs
2 teaspoons vanilla
3 tablespoons water
4 cups flour
2 teaspoons baking
  powder
2 teaspoons salt
2 teaspoons baking
  soda

2 cups white chocolate
  chips
2 cups semisweet
  chocolate chips
3 cups raisins
3 cups chopped nuts
2 cups old-fashioned
  rolled oats
3 cups orange almond
  granola (or any good
  granola mixed with 3
  teaspoons grated
  orange rind)

Blend butter and sugars until creamy. Then add eggs, vanilla and water. Beat until well-mixed. Sift together flour, baking powder, salt and baking soda. Stir into egg and butter mixture and mix until just blended. Then add remaining ingredients. When well-mixed, shape into ping pong or golf ball size balls and bake on an ungreased cookie sheet at 350° for 8 to 10 minutes or until just turning brown around the edges. Best when warm from the oven. Dough keeps refrigerated or frozen. Bake them fresh as needed. My cookies were featured once in *Family Circle Magazine* and Rose Leavy Buranbaum's *Christmas Cookie Book*. In the last year that I had the Babbling Brook Inn, over 9,000 cookies were baked for my guests. Enjoy!

Submitted by Highland Inn of San Juan Island, Friday Harbor

www.wbbg.com

♥ Mt. Rainier Snowball Cookies ♥

2 cups sifted all purpose
  flour
3/4 teaspoon salt
1 cup (2 sticks) butter,
  room temperature, do
  not use margarine
1/2 cup granulated sugar

1 teaspoon vanilla
1 cup finely chopped
  pecans
3/4 cup sifted
  confectioners sugar
1 bag Hershey® chocolate
  kisses

Preheat oven to 325°. Butter 2 baking sheets. Onto a piece of waxed paper, sift flour and salt. In medium size bowl with an electric mixer on high, cream butter and granulated sugar until light and fluffy; beat in vanilla. Using a wooden spoon stir in flour mixture, then pecans. Dust your hands with a little of the confectioners sugar and roll dough into 1" balls. Place 2" apart on baking sheets. Press a chocolate kiss into the center of each cookie, flattening dough slightly. Bake for 25 minutes or just until golden brown. Transfer to rack to cool for 15 minutes. Sprinkle the top of each cookie with confectioners sugar. Makes about 3 dozen cookies. If any are ever left, which I doubt there will be, these cookies will keep for up to 2 weeks in an airtight container, but they do not freeze well.

Submitted by The Rose of Gig Harbor, a B&B Inn, Gig Harbor

♥ Oatmeal Tea Cookies ♥

1 cup softened butter
1 cup sugar
1 1/2 cups flour

1 3/4 cups quick oats
1 teaspoon baking
  soda

Cream butter and sugar in bowl. Add remaining ingredients. Mix together. Drop 1" dough balls on greased cookie sheet. Bake at 350° for 12 minutes. Let cool before removing from cookie sheet. Can be rolled in powdered sugar when cooled. Makes 24 - 2" cookies.

Submitted by A Harbor View B&B, Aberdeen

♥ Orange-Flavored Gingerbread Boys ♥

1/3 cup margarine
1 cup brown sugar
1 cup molasses
1/2 cup honey
1/2 cup orange juice
  concentrate
1/4 cup water

7 cups flour
2 teaspoons baking soda
1/4 teaspoon salt
1 teaspoon allspice
1 teaspoon ginger
1 teaspoon cloves
1 teaspoon cinnamon

Beat together margarine, brown sugar, molasses and honey. Stir in orange juice concentrate and water. Blend all dry ingredients together. Stir dry into wet ingredients. Chill dough for at least 30 minutes until firm. Preheat oven to 350°. Roll dough approximately 1/4" thick on floured surface and cut out shapes with floured cookie cutters. Use 2 small red cinnamon candies for boys' buttons. Bake on lightly greased cookie sheets for approximately 10 minutes. Makes about 2 1/2 dozen cookies.

Submitted by The FARMHOUSE, Whidbey Island - Langley

♥ Peanut Butter Chocolate Cookies ♥

1 cup shortening
3/4 - 1 cup peanut butter,
  to taste
1 cup brown sugar,
  packed
1/2 cup sugar
3 eggs
3 teaspoons vanilla
  extract

2 cups flour
2 teaspoons baking
  powder
2 cups oatmeal
12 ounces chocolate
  chips
Coconut, salted peanuts,
  and raisins (opt.)

In large mixing bowl cream together shortening, peanut butter, brown sugar, and sugar. Add eggs and vanilla extract; beat until fluffy. Sift flour and baking powder, add to creamed mixture and blend well. Stir in oatmeal, chocolate chips, plus coconut, peanuts, or raisins, if used. Place on greased cookie sheets; make cookies any size you want. Bake at 350° for 10 to 12 minutes. Makes 2 dozen cookies.

Submitted by Peacock Hill Guest House, Gig Harbor Area

♥   # Peanut Butter Cookies   ♥

1 egg
1 cup sugar
1 cup peanut
  butter

May top with a chocolate
  kiss, roll in crushed
  nuts, or add chocolate
  or butterscotch chips

Mix egg, sugar and peanut butter well. Drop on ungreased cookie sheet and flatten with a criss-cross of fork tines. May be topped with a chocolate kiss, rolled in crushed nuts, or add chocolate or butterscotch chips, if desired. Bake at 350° for 8 to 10 minutes. Makes 2 1/2 dozen cookies.

Submitted by Chelsea Station on the Park, Seattle

♥   # Peanut Butter Oatmeal Cookies   ♥

1 cup margarine
1 cup peanut butter
1 cup sugar
3/4 cup brown sugar
2 eggs
1 teaspoon vanilla

2 cups quick oats
1 1/4 cups flour
1 teaspoon baking
  powder
1 teaspoon baking soda
3/4 cup chocolate chips

With mixer beat margarine and peanut butter. Mix in sugars, eggs, and vanilla; add to dry ingredients. Add chocolate chips. Drop by spoonfuls onto ungreased cookie sheet. Bake at 350° for 10 - 12 minutes.

Submitted by DeVoe Mansion, Tacoma

♥ # Rich Shortbread ♥

1 1/2 cups all purpose
  flour
1/2 cup sweet butter,
  cubed

5 - 6 tablespoons
  sugar
1 egg yolk,
  lightly beaten

Preheat oven to 350° and lightly butter an 8" square nonstick pan. Rub together flour and butter until sand-like in texture, then add 4 tablespoons of sugar and mix well. With a fork, mix in egg yolk to form a rough, dryish paste. Press mixture evenly in pan. Prick with a fork evenly in rows. Sprinkle with remaining sugar. Bake for 20 minutes; then reduce oven heat to 200° and continue baking for 50 minutes. Cut into 1" x 2" fingers while still warm. Leave to cool completely in the pan.

Submitted by Channel House, Anacortes

♥ # South Bay Signature Cookies ♥

1 cup butter or margarine
1 cup granulated sugar
2 eggs
1 cup cooking oil

1 cup powdered sugar
1 teaspoon cream of tartar
1 teaspoon baking soda
4 cups flour

Cream butter and sugar until light and fluffy. Add eggs one at a time. Add cooking oil and mix well. Add powdered sugar, mix well. Add cream of tartar and baking soda to flour. Add flour one cup at a time. Mix well. Using a teaspoon, place walnut size drops on ungreased cookie sheets. Press each slightly with a sugar-dipped glass. Bake at 350° for 7 minutes. Do not overbake. Immediately press with cookie press to imprint. Remove to cooling racks.

Submitted by South Bay B&B, Lake Whatcom - Sedro Woolley

♥ Stratford Oatmeal Chip Cookies ♥

1 cup shortening
1 cup sugar
1 cup packed brown sugar
2 eggs
1/4 cup molasses
1 teaspoon vanilla

1 teaspoon baking soda
1 1/2 cups flour
3 cups quick-cooking oatmeal
1 cup chocolate chips
1/2 cup raisins

Cream together shortening and sugars. Add eggs, molasses, and vanilla. Add baking soda and flour. Mix well. Stir in oatmeal, chocolate chips, and raisins. Bake at 350° for 8 to 10 minutes.

Submitted by Stratford Manor, Bellingham

♥ The Guest House B&B Shortbread ♥

1/4 cup + 1 tablespoon sugar, divided
3 tablespoons cornstarch

1 1/4 cups flour
1/2 cup cold butter, cut into pieces

Place 1/4 cup sugar, cornstarch, flour and butter in mixing bowl. With your fingertips rub butter into dry ingredients until crumbly and no large particles remain. Form mixture into a ball and place in an ungreased 8" or 9" round cake pan. Firmly press dough into an even layer. With the tines of a fork, make impressions around the outside edge of the dough, and then prick the center surface evenly. Bake at 325° for approximately 40 minutes. While still hot cut into pie wedges. Sprinkle with an additional 1 tablespoon sugar. Cool completely before removing from cake pan. Makes 8 - 12 wedges.

Submitted by The Guest House B&B, Seattle

Food Allergy Substitutions

To substitute milk - use equivalent amounts of one of the following:

- Orange juice
- Apple juice
- Soy milk
- Other fruit juice
- Broth, such as chicken or beef
- Zucchini water - 1/2 to 1 cup water to 1 whole zucchini (1/2 cup for small zucchini and 1 cup for large zucchini). Peel and remove seeds, blend in a blender until smooth and milky in appearance.

To substitute for 1 cup wheat flour where a starch is the main ingredient such as breads, muffins, cakes, pies, etc. - use one of the following:

- 3/4 cup rice flour
- 1 1/3 cups oat flour
- 1 1/4 cups rye flour
- 1 cup rye meal (flour)
- 1 cup barley flour
- 1 cup corn flour
- 3/4 cup cornmeal (coarse)
- 1 scant cup cornmeal (fine)
- 5/8 cup potato starch flour (10 tablespoons)

To substitute for 1 tablespoon wheat flour when using flour as a thickener for puddings and pie fillings - use one of the following:

- 1 tablespoon cornstarch
- 1 tablespoon tapioca starch
- 2/3 tablespoon rice flour
- 2/3 tablespoon arrowroot flour
- 2/3 tablespoon potato starch
- 1 tablespoon poi

To substitute for 1 tablespoon cornstarch as thickener (same as above) - use the following:

- 2/3 tablespoon arrowroot flour
- 2/3 tablespoon potato starch
- 1 tablespoon poi
- 2/3 tablespoon rice flour
- 1 tablespoon wheat flour
- 1 tablespoon tapioca starch or minute tapioca

Food Allergy Substitutions (Con't.)

Substitutes for corn oil in baked goods:

- safflower
- sunflower
- sesame
- peanut
- cottonseed

Substitutes for butter or margarine:

- a soy based butter or margarine which does not contain dairy products
- safflower sticks
- solid shortening - such as Crisco® which does not contain corn or dairy products (always check ingredient labels)
- Mazola® margarine - does not contain dairy but does contain corn oil

Other Substitutions

• 1 cup sugar	1 1/3 cups brown sugar or 1 1/2 cups powdered sugar
• 1 cup honey	1 1/4 cups sugar and 1/4 cup liquid
• 1 cup brown sugar	1 cup granulated sugar and 2 tablespoons molasses
• 1 cup powdered sugar	1 cup sugar and 1 tablespoon cornstarch (blend in blender)
• 1 cup milk	1/2 cup evaporated milk plus 1/2 cup water or 1/4 cup nonfat dry milk plus 7/8 cup water plus 2 teaspoons butter
• 1 cup buttermilk	1 tablespoon vinegar or lemon juice plus milk to make 1 cup. Let stand 5 minutes. Or 1 cup yogurt
• 1 cup sour milk	1 tablespoon vinegar or lemon juice or 1 3/4 teaspoons cream of tartar plus 1 cup sweet milk
• 1 cup half and half	7/8 cup milk plus 1/2 tablespoon butter or 1/2 cup coffee creamer and 1/2 cup milk
• 1 cup sour cream	1 cup cottage cheese, 1 - 3 tablespoons milk, 1 tablespoon lemon juice. Blend; store in refrigerator.

Guide To Measures

- Dash = less than 1/8 teaspoon
- 3 teaspoons = 1 tablespoon
- 2 tablespoons = 1 ounce
- 4 tablespoons = 1/4 cup
- 5 1/3 tablespoons = 1/3 cup
- 8 tablespoons = 1/2 cup
- 10 2/3 tablespoons = 2/3 cup
- 12 tablespoons = 3/4 cup
- 14 tablespoons = 7/8 cup
- 16 tablespoons = 1 cup
- 1 cup = 1/2 pint
- 2 cups = 1 pint
- 4 cups = 2 pints or 1 quart
- 4 quarts = 1 gallon
- 16 ounces = 1 pound

Guide To Equivalents

- 1 pound butter = 2 cups
- 1 stick butter = 1/2 cup
- 1 pound granulated sugar = 2 cups
- 1 pound brown sugar = 2 1/2 cups
- 1 pound powdered sugar = 3 1/2 cups
- 1 square chocolate = 1 ounce or 3 tablespoons grated
- 1 average size lemon = 3 tablespoons juice
- 5 - 8 average size lemons = 1 cup juice
- 1 lemon rind, grated = 1 tablespoon
- 1 orange = 2 - 3 tablespoons juice
- 1 orange rind, grated = 2 tablespoons
- 3 medium oranges = 1 cup juice

Average Contents Of Standard Cans

- 8 ounce can = 1 cup
- No. 300 can = 1 3/4 cups
- No. 1 tall can = 2 cups
- No. 303 can = 2 cups
- No. 2 can = 2 1/2 cups
- No. 2 1/2 can = 3 1/2 cups
- No. 3 can = 4 cups
- No. 5 can = 7 1/4 cups
- No. 10 can = 13 cups

Index of Recipes

Washington State Map

When Making Reservations . . .

• Advance Reservations Recommended

In order not to be disappointed, please call ahead to reserve your Bed and Breakfast stay. Many of our B&Bs are booked in advance, especially on three-day weekends and during the summer months. If you would like to schedule a Bed and Breakfast for a special getaway, (i.e. anniversary, birthday, etc.) you will want to call early. (This could mean several weeks to several months ahead depending on the popularity of the B&B you've selected.)

• Deposits / Cancellation Policies / Special Needs

Some B&Bs accept credit cards to hold a reservation. Others require an advance deposit by check.

Discuss cancellation policies ahead of time. If you need to cancel, do so at the earliest possible time. B&Bs are small operations and do not overbook. If you cancel a reservation, there may be a fee if the room cannot be booked again.

Please inform your host of any special needs that you may have, including any dietary restrictions.

• Arrival Time

You will probably be asked for an expected arrival time. Most B&Bs do not maintain a 24-hour desk and typically set aside a window of time for check in. If you plan to arrive later or earlier, call ahead just as if you were visiting a friend. Your courtesy will be greatly appreciated.

Washington Bed & Breakfast Guild Gift Certificate

Never know what to buy for your Mom or Dad?

Have a friend who needs a getaway and you would like to give them

freedom to choose the destination?

Need a wedding present that will keep on giving long after it is used?

Are you a Grandma and need an excuse to babysit the grand-kids?

The Washington Bed & Breakfast Guild has the answer.

A Washington Bed & Breakfast Guild Gift Certificate!

You purchase certificates in denominations of $25 and present them to your friend or loved one. They use them just like cash at any of over 100 Washington Bed & Breakfast Guild member inns. The certificates never expire and the number of member inns accepting the certificates grows each day.

Order your certificates today by calling 800-647-2918 or

at our web site www.wbbg.com

Aberdeen

1908 COONEY MANSION

1705 Fifth Street (Box 54)   360-533-0602
Cosmopolis, WA 98537   800-411-6462
Judi & Jim Lohr
E-mail: cooney@cooneymansion.com
www.cooneymansion.com
Award winning loggers' breakfast • Secluded • Historic Register • Private baths •
Spa • Sauna • Fireplaces • Golf • Tennis • Gateway to Olympics, beach • Afternoon
tea • Workout room • *Northwest Best Places.*

A HARBOR VIEW B&B

111 West 11th Street   360-533-7996
Aberdeen, WA 98520   877-533-7996
Cindy Lonn   360-533-0433 FAX
E-mail: harborview@olynet.com
www.aharborview.com
Every room with water and mountain views • Historic 1905 Colonial home •
Country Breakfast • Private baths • TV • Phone • Nearby rainforest and beaches •
Historic homes walking tour included.

Anacortes

ALBATROSS B&B

5708 Kingsway   360-293-0677
Anacortes, WA 98221   800-622-8864
Linda & Lorrie Flowers   360-299-2232 FAX
E-mail: albatros@cnw.com
http://www.cnw.com/~albatros
Historic 1927 home adjacent to beach/park/marina • Views of islands & mountains
• 4 rooms • Private baths • Full meal • K/Q beds • Art & antiques • Near San Juan
ferry • Whale watching • Fishing.

CHANNEL HOUSE

2902 Oakes Avenue   360-293-9382
Anacortes, WA 98221   800-238-4353
Dennis & Patricia McIntyre   360-299-9208 FAX
E-mail: beds@sos.net
www.channel-house.com
1902 Craftsman home, 1 3/4 mi. to ferry • Waterview, fireplaces, private baths and
full breakfast • End your day with cookies and coffee or stargaze from hot tub • *NW
Best Places* and "Places to Kiss."

Anacortes (Con't.)

NANTUCKET INN

3402 Commercial Avenue
Anacortes, WA 98221
Lynda & Doug Bransford, Owners
E-mail: nantucketinn@halcyon.com
www.whidbey.com/nantucket

360-293-6007
888-293-6007
360-299-4339 FAX

Colonial style home • Built in 1925 • Located on a hill above town with fantastic views of Mount Baker and Fidalgo Bay • 5 guest rooms • Full breakfasts • Fine dining on premises Thursday through Sunday.

OLD BROOK INN

7270 Old Brook Lane
Anacortes, WA 98221
Dick Ash

360-293-4768
800-503-4768
360-299-9720 FAX

Children and pets welcome • Private bathrooms • Queen beds • Walking trails plus a babbling brook and trout pond set on 9 acres of peaceful seclusion • Golfing nearby.

Belfair

SELAH INN

130 N.E. Dulalip Landing
Belfair, WA 98528
Bonnie & Pat McCullough
E-mail: innkeeper@selahinn.com
www.selahinn.com

360-275-0916
877-232-7941
360-277-3187 FAX

Elegant Northwest lodge on gorgeous Hood Canal • Full breakfast • Dinner by reservation • King & queen rooms with private baths • Fireplace, whirlpool • Deck spa • Golf, bike, kayak, beach fun • "Best Places to Kiss" • *Romantic America Northwest* • AAA.

Bellingham

SCHNAUZER CROSSING

4421 Lakeway Drive
Bellingham, WA 98226
Vermont & Donna McAllister
E-mail: Schnauzerx@aol.com
www.schnauzercrossing.com

360-734-2808
800-562-2808
360-734-2808 FAX

Lake Whatcom's luxury B&B • Garden suite has fireplace and jacuzzi tub • Queen bedroom has lake view and private bath • Cottage in 100' trees • Fresh flowers • Down comforters • Lavish breakfast • Outdoor spa • 1 1/2 acres of gardens with Japanese teahouse and meditation garden, koi pond.

Bellingham (Con't.)

STRATFORD MANOR

4566 Anderson Way   360-715-8441
Bellingham, WA 98226   800-240-6779
Leslie & Jim Lohse   360-671-0840 FAX
E-mail: llohse@aol.com
www.stratfordmanor.com
Comfortably luxurious Tudor style home on 30 acres • Countryside views • King & queen beds • Fireplaces • Private baths with jetted tubs • Fresh flowers • Fruit baskets • Cookies • Hot tub on deck • Full breakfast.

Bremerton

ILLAHEE MANOR B&B

6680 Illahee Road N.E.   360-698-7555
Bremerton, WA 98311   800-693-6680
Case Family LLC, Owners   360-698-0688 FAX
Jeff & Dorée Pratt, Innkeepers
E-mail: innkeeper@illaheemanor.com
www.illaheemanor.com
A 1920's waterfront manor house with 5 luxurious suites and 2 detached cabins • Whirlpool tubs • Water views • Fireplaces • Llama and deer • Three-course breakfast prepared by our in-house chef.

Camano Island

INN AT BARNUM POINT

464 South Barnum Road   360-387-2256
Camano Island, WA 98282   800-910-2256
Carolin Barnum Dilorenzo   360-387-2256 FAX
E-mail: barnum@camano.net
www.whidbey.com/inn/
Secluded beach hideaway • Spectacular view • Spacious rooms with private baths • Fireplaces, down quilts, hearty breakfast • Watch eagles soar, deer graze, otters fish • Near golf, state park and hiking trails.

PEIFFERHAUS B&B

1462 East Larkspur Lane   360-629-4746
Camano Island, WA 98292   877-623-8497
Mary Ann Peiffer   360-629-4785 FAX
E-mail: tom@greatnorthern.net
peifferhaus.com
Relax in country-like setting • Water and mountain views • Creatively decorated rooms • Private baths • Gourmet breakfast, espresso • Close to Stanwood • Beautiful grounds on 5 acres.

Cathlamet

THE BRADLEY HOUSE

P.O. Box 35 - 61 Main Street   360-795-3030
Cathlamet, WA 98612   800-551-1691
Barbara & Tony West
E-mail: bradleyhouse@transport.com
Beautifully preserved 1907 Eastlake home overlooking the Columbia River • 4 lovely rooms, 2 with private bath • Walk to restaurants • Near marina, game refuge, museums • Fodor's • *NW Best Places* • Full breakfast.

Concrete-Birdsview

CASCADE MOUNTAIN INN

40418 Pioneer Lane   360-826-4333
Concrete-Birdsview, WA 98237   888-652-8127
Sally & John Brummett   360-826-3623 FAX
E-mail: casmi1@gte.net
www.cascade-mtn-inn.com
Enjoy the casual elegance of our country Inn • Five unique guest rooms, all with private baths • Full breakfast • Mountain views & Skagit River nearby • Outdoor hot tub • Romantic getaway • 1 1/2 hours from Seattle.

Darrington

MT. HIGGINS HOUSE

29805 S.R. 530 N.E.   360-435-8703
Arlington, WA 98223   888-296-3777
Renee Ottersen   360-435-9757 FAX
E-mail: mthigginshouse@juno.com
Secluded retreat on 70-acre historic farm • All rooms with mountain view • River rock fireplace • Large deck overlooks trout pond • Enjoy birding, fishing and hiking • River access • Private bath • Adults • Smoke free.

Ellensburg

CAMPUS VIEW INN

706 North Anderson Street   509-933-2345
Ellensburg, WA 98926   800-428-7270
Diana Oltman   509-962-9135 FAX
E-mail: elegance@campusviewinn.com
campusviewinn.com
Elegant 1910 Victorian next to CWU Campus • 5 guest rooms with private baths • Queen beds • Soaking tub • Fireplace • TV • Fridge • Snacks • Farm breakfast • Down comforters • Theme rooms • Near shops.

Enumclaw

THE WHITE ROSE INN

1610 Griffin Avenue
Enumclaw, WA 98022
Eleanor Ludwig, Owner
Tami & Michael Dunn, Innkeepers
E-mail: innkeepr@whiteroseinnbb.com
www.whiteroseinnbb.com

360-825-7194
800-404-7194
360-802-2472 FAX

Elegant 1922 Colonial mansion • Period furnishings • Large rooms • Private baths
• Full breakfasts • Near Mount Rainier and Crystal Mountain • Skiing and hiking •
A beautiful place for a wedding or reception.

Everett

GAYLORD HOUSE

3301 Grand Avenue
Everett, WA 98201
Gaylord, Shirley Anne & Theresa Schaudies
E-mail: gaylord_house@msn.com

425-339-9153
888-507-7177
425-303-9713 FAX

Gracious old home and hosts • Tree-lined street, walk to downtown • Scrumptious
breakfasts, bottomless cookie jars and fruit bowl • 5 rooms, queen and twin beds,
private baths • Air-conditioning, TV/VCR, phones, mountain view.

Federal Way

KILLARNEY COVE B&B

2860 South 354th Lane
Federal Way, WA 98003
Paul & Fran Morris, Owners
Ryan & Bethany Morris, Innkeepers
E-mail: killarneycove@seanet.com
www.killarneycove.com

253-838-4595
253-838-4595 FAX

Quiet, peaceful lakeside home • "So near, yet so far away" • 3 rooms with private
baths • Full breakfast • Queen beds • TV/VCR • Living room fireplace • Decks •
Fishing poles • Non-smoking.

Forks

MILLER TREE INN

P.O. Box 1565 (mailing)
654 East Division Street
Forks, WA 98331
Bill & Susan Brager
E-mail: millertreeinn@centurytel.net
www.millertreeinn.com

360-374-6806
800-943-6563
360-374-6807 FAX

1916 historic farmhouse near Hoh Rainforest • Pacific beaches • Hot tub • 7 cozy
rooms • Full breakfast • Private and shared baths • Spacious grounds • 13 years
listed in *NW Best Places* • MC/Visa.

Gig Harbor Area

BEACHSIDE B&B

679 Kamus Drive   253-549-2524
Fox Island, WA 98333   253-549-2524 FAX
Doreen Samuelson
www.beachsidebb.com
Beachcomber's paradise • Magnificent view of Cascades and sunsets • Hot tub •
Private entrances • Cozy English decor • Wood fireplace • Cable • Kitchen •
Continental breakfast • Spacious • Gold Seal Award.

THE FOUNTAINS B&B

926 - 120th Street N.W.   253-851-6262
Gig Harbor, WA 98332
Meri Fountain
E-mail: merifountain@aol.com
http://fountainsbb.com
Delight in the Puget Sound view from your suite with private entrance and bath •
TV • Phone • Refrigerator • Queen bed • Decadent breakfasts selected from a menu
of NW favorites • Warm hospitality • MC/Visa.

ISLAND ESCAPE B&B

210 Island Boulevard   253-549-2044
Fox Island, WA 98333   877-549-2044
Paula E. Pascoe
E-mail: paula@island-escape.com
www.island-escape.com
Private suite for 2 with mountain/water views • Fireplace • Private deck, entrance,
jacuzzi bath • Full breakfast • Restaurant discounts • Gig Harbor 10 minutes via
bridge • Superb service • Recommended in *Pacific Northwest Magazine*.

PEACOCK HILL GUEST HOUSE

9520 Peacock Hill Avenue   800-863-2318
Gig Harbor, WA 98332
Suzanne & Steve Savlov
E-mail: SedonaSue@aol.com
www.virtualcities.com/wa/peacock.html
Nestled among evergreens, sitting on a hilltop overlooking the harbor • Sit back
and enjoy all of the comforts of home in Salish Suite or Sedona Room • Stroll
down to the harbor and shops • Gourmet breakfast.

THE ROSE OF GIG HARBOR, A B&B INN

3202 Harborview Drive   253-853-7990
Gig Harbor, WA 98335   877-640-7673
Morton & Nancy Altman   253-853-7992 FAX
E-mail: mnaltman@harbornet.com
On the waterfront in the heart of the city, the "Rose" is an ideal getaway • This
historic 1917 home has been lovingly restored to accommodate both vacation and
business travelers.

Gig Harbor Area (Con't.)

WATER'S EDGE B&B

8610 Goodman Drive N.W.   253-851-3891
Gig Harbor, WA 98332   253-857-6950 FAX
Joanie & Paul Mann
E-mail: mannpj@gateway.net
Enjoy the quiet charm of Gig Harbor from a private waterfront suite on Gig Harbor Bay • Close to town • Living room with gas fireplace • Bedroom • Private bath • Separate entrance • Outdoor spa • Dock.

La Conner (Mt. Vernon)

KATY'S INN

P.O. Box 869 - 503 South Third   360-466-3366
La Conner, WA 98257   800-914-7767
Bruce & Kathie Hubbard
http://home.ncia.com/katysinn/
Charming 1882 Victorian nestled on hillside 2 blocks above quaint La Conner • 4 lovely rooms/2 suites • All private baths • Evening snack • Gazebo with hot tub • Full breakfast • "Best Places to Kiss."

SAMISH POINT BY THE BAY

4465 Samish Point Road   360-766-6610
Bow, WA 98232   800-916-6161
Herb & Theresa Goldston   360-766-6610 FAX
E-mail: hgtg@samishpoint.com
A private Cape Cod cottage with woodland and garden views on 33 waterfront acres • Charming decor, well-stocked pantry, stone fireplace hot tub, king & queen beds • "Best Places to Kiss" • *NW Best Places.*

SKAGIT BAY HIDEAWAY

P.O. Box 497 - 17430 Goldenview Avenue   360-466-2262
La Conner, WA 98257   888-466-2262
Earlene Beckes & Kevin Haberly   360-466-7493 FAX
E-mail: hideaway@skagitbay.com
www.skagitbay.com
Cross La Conner's Rainbow Bridge to a special island waterfront getaway • Relax by the fire in your cozy living room • Luxuriate in your multi-spray shower • Soak in your private rooftop spa • Spectacular sunsets.

WHITE SWAN GUEST HOUSE

15872 Moore Road   360-445-6805
Mt. Vernon, WA 98273
Peter Goldfarb
A storybook Victorian farmhouse • 3 cozy rooms • 2 baths to share • Separate romantic cottage • Country-continental breakfast • Chocolate-chip cookies • As seen in *Country Home Magazine* • 6 miles to La Conner.

Lake Whatcom

SOUTH BAY B&B

4095 South Bay Drive / Lake Whatcom
Sedro Woolley, WA 98284
Dan & Sally Moore
E-mail: southbay@gte.net
www.southbaybb.com

360-595-2086
877-595-2086
360-595-1043 FAX

Classic Craftsman lakeside retreat • 5 view rooms with private baths • Private patios • Down comforters • Ironed linens • Whirlpool tubs for two • Gas fireplaces • Sunroom • Wraparound porch • Beach access • Full breakfast.

Leavenworth

ALL SEASONS RIVER INN

P.O. Box 788 - 8751 Icicle Road
Leavenworth, WA 98826
Kathy & Jeff Falconer
E-mail: info@allseasonsriverinn.com
www.allseasonsriverinn.com

509-548-1425
800-254-0555

Sleep lulled by the river • Awaken to gourmet breakfast • Spacious river-view rooms and 2-room suites • All with jacuzzi or fireplace • Private deck • Antiques • Bikes • Near town • Adults • Non-smoking.

AUTUMN POND B&B

10388 Titus Road
Leavenworth, WA 98826
John & Jennifer Lorenz
E-mail: info@autumnpond.com
www.autumnpond.com

509-548-4482
800-222-9661

Majestic mountain views on 3 quiet acres with fish and duck pond • Walk to town • Moonlight hot tub • Private baths • Non-smoking • Large living area with pellet stove • Full breakfast • 5 rooms • Groups welcome.

BOSCH GÄRTEN B&B

9846 Dye Road
Leavenworth, WA 98826
Georgeanne & Denny Nichols
E-mail: innkeeper@boschgarten.com
www.boschgarten.com

509-548-6900
800-535-0069
509-548-3610 FAX

Quiet elegance • Lovely gardens • Mountain views • Large airy rooms • Private baths • King beds • Decks • Full breakfast • Fireplace • Enclosed hot tub • Walk to village • Cable TV • Non-smoking • Bicycles.

Leavenworth (Con't.)

RUN OF THE RIVER

P.O. Box 285 - 9308 East Leavenworth Road   509-548-7171
Leavenworth, WA 98826   800-288-6491
Monty & Karen Turner
E-mail: info@runoftheriver.com
runoftheriver.com
Suppose Martha Stewart and Eddie Bauer buddied up to "do" an inn? • You would get lots of laughter, romance and all the details properly tended • Then you would get a massage for two • A Northwest tradition.

Long Beach Peninsula

BOREAS B&B INN

P.O. Box 1344 - 607 North Ocean Beach Blvd.   360-642-8069
Long Beach, WA 98631   888-642-8069
Susie Goldsmith & Bill Verner   360-642-5353 FAX
E-mail: boreas@boreasinn.com
www.boreasinn.com
Ocean-front luxury • 1920's fantasy beachhouse • Gardens • Dunes • Spa • 5 guest rooms with private baths, 1 with spa • Delectable brunch • Walk to shops and boardwalk • "Best Places to Kiss" • *NW Best Places*.

SCANDINAVIAN GARDENS INN

1610 California Avenue S.W.   360-642-8877
Long Beach, WA 98631   800-988-9277
Rod & Marilyn Dakan   360-642-8764 FAX
E-mail: sginn@longbeachwa.com
Be pampered with our touch of Scandinavia • 4 rooms and a 2-room honeymoon suite with soaking tub • Private baths • 5-course gourmet breakfast • Homemade pastries • AAA • *NW Best Places*.

THE WHALEBONE HOUSE

2101 Bay Avenue   360-665-5371
Ocean Park, WA 98640   888-298-3330
Jim & Jayne Nash
E-mail: whalebone@willapabay.org
willapabay.org/~whalebone
1889 Victorian farmhouse on WA Historical Register • 4 rooms with private baths • Queen beds • Fresh Northwest breakfast • Sunporch, deck, gardens • Antiques & beach whimsy • Close to ocean & Willapa Bay • Northwest "Best Places to Kiss."

Olalla

CHILDS' HOUSE B&B

8331 S.E. Willock Road   253-857-4252
Olalla, WA 98359   800-250-4954
Susan Childs
E-mail: childshse@aol.com
users.aol.com/childshse/BnB.htm
3 Country Victorian rooms • Master suite with king bed, soaking bath, private deck • Ideal romantic escape • Gourmet meals • Weddings • Retreats • Catering • 15 minutes from Gig Harbor.

Point Roberts

MAPLE MEADOW B&B

101 Goodman Road   360-945-5536
Point Roberts, WA 98281   360-945-2855 FAX
Terrie & Keith LaPorte
E-mail: mplmedbb@whidbey.com
Historic 1910 farmhouse on 5 acres • Furnished with antiques • Offers unique getaway, close to ferry and international airport • Surrounded by water, hiking & bicycle trails • Birdwatching haven • Full breakfast.

Port Angeles

ANGELES INN

P.O. Box 87 - 1203 East 7th Street   360-417-0260
Port Angeles, WA 98362   888-552-4263
Al & June James   360-457-4269 FAX
E-mail: james@olypen.com
Modern contemporary dwelling • Quiet location • 4 spacious ground level rooms, 2 with private baths • All have king beds • 10 minutes to Olympic National Park & Victoria, British Columbia ferries • Smoke free • TV • Phones.

BJ'S GARDEN GATE

397 Monterra Drive   360-452-2322
Port Angeles, WA 98362   800-880-1332
BJ & Frank Paton   360-417-5098 FAX
E-mail: bjgarden@olypen.com
bjgarden.com
Waterfront Victorian estate • Pamper yourself with private fireplace, bathroom, jacuzzi for 2, antique king and queen bed and a panoramic water view • TV, VCR and CD • Full savory breakfast.

Port Angeles (Con't.)

TUDOR INN

1108 South Oak
Port Angeles, WA 98362
Jane Glass
E-mail: info@tudorinn.com
www.tudorinn.com

360-452-3138

Award-winning Old English style with antiques • Garden, water and mountain views • Close to ferry and park • Full breakfast • 5 rooms, 1 with fireplace • All private baths • *NW Best Places* • AAA • Mobil • "Best Places to Kiss."

Port Orchard

"REFLECTIONS" - A B&B INN

3878 Reflection Lane East
Port Orchard, WA 98366
Jim & Cathy Hall
E-mail: jimreflect@hurricane.net

360-871-5582

Water views from 3 rooms & suite, two with private baths • New England antiques • Full gourmet breakfast • Romantic hot tub • Day trips to Seattle, Olympic Peninsula • Marinas, antiques nearby • *NW Best Places*.

Port Townsend

RAVENSCROFT INN

533 Quincy Street
Port Townsend, WA 98368
Tim & Gay Stover
E-mail: ravenscroft@olympus.net

360-385-2784
800-782-2691
360-385-6724 FAX

"Lasting memories" • 8 luxury rooms • Soaking tubs • Fireplaces • Sweeping water views • Full breakfast • "Quintessential pampering" • 50 Romantic Getaways • "Best Places to Kiss" • *NW Best Places* .

Poulsbo

FOXBRIDGE B&B

30680 Hwy. 3 N.E.
Poulsbo, WA 98370
Beverly Higgins

360-598-5599

This beautiful Georgian Manor rests on five secluded acres in a tranquil country setting • Wildlife, birds and a trout pond • Exquisite rooms with private baths • Gourmet breakfast included.

Roslyn

HUMMINGBIRD INN

P.O. Box 984 - 106 Pennsylvania Avenue East   509-649-2758
Roslyn, WA 98941
Roberta Spinazola
E-mail: jabo@eburg.com
http://blueplanet-group.com/hummingbirdinn
Hummingbirds abound • Circa 1890's Victorian home set in historic Roslyn • Clawfoot tub • Fireplace • Piano • Queen size beds • Full breakfast • Year round recreational activities • MC/Visa/Discover.

Salkum

THE SHEPHERD'S INN B&B

168 Autumn Heights Drive   360-985-2434
Salkum, WA 98582   800-985-2434
Richard & Ellen Berdan
E-mail: shepherd@theshepherdsinn.com
theshepherdsinn.com
Between Mt. St. Helen's & Mt. Rainier • 50 mile sunset views • 40+ tranquil wooded acres • Wildlife • Huckleberry crepes! • Private baths • Private double jacuzzi • Smoke free • Fireplace • MC/Visa/Discover/Am Ex.

THE SAN JUAN ISLANDS

Lopez Island

EDENWILD INN

P.O. Box 271   360-468-3238
132 Lopez Road   800-606-0662
Lopez Island, WA 98261   360-468-4080 FAX
Mary-Anne Miller & Clark Haley
E-mail: edenwildinn@msn.com
www.edenwildinn.com
Discover our elegant, yet friendly, Victorian Inn • Stroll to shops, restaurants and galleries in picturesque Lopez Village • Experience our renowned country breakfast and first class service.

Orcas Island

BUCK BAY FARM

716 Point Lawrence Road   360-376-2908
Olga, WA 98279   888-422-2825
Rick & Janet Bronkey
www.buckbayfarm.com
Warm farmhouse hospitality • Pastoral views • Sunroom • Deck • Cozy rooms with private baths • Hearty homestyle breakfast • Near Moran State Park hiking trails and the beach • Spa.

Orcas Island (Con't.)

KANGAROO HOUSE B&B ON ORCAS ISLAND

P.O. Box 334   360-376-2175
Eastsound, WA 98245   888-371-2175
Helen & Peter Allen   360-376-3604 FAX
E-mail: innkeeper@kangaroohouse.com
www.kangaroohouse.com
1907 Craftsman-style home with large fireplace • Walking distance to Eastsound Village • Private and shared baths • Families welcome • Delicious full breakfast • Casual comfort • Garden hot tub.

THE ORCAS HOTEL

P.O. Box 155   360-376-4300
Orcas, WA 98280   360-376-4399 FAX
Laura & Doug Tidwell
E-mail: orcas@orcashotel.com
The Orcas Hotel is a restored Victorian Inn listed on the National Register of Historic Places • It greets all who arrive on Orcas by ferry and is the perfect place to begin your island adventures.

OTTERS POND B&B OF ORCAS ISLAND

P.O. Box 1540   360-376-8844
Eastsound, WA 98245   888-893-9680
Carl & Susan Silvernail   360-376-8847 FAX
E-mail: silvernl@ix.netcom.com
www.otterspond.com
Beautiful Bed & Breakfast on 20-acre pond • French Country elegance • King and queen beds • 5-course sumptuous breakfast • Naturalist's paradise bordering Moran State Park • Easy access to Orcas Island artists, shopping and activities.

WINDSONG INN

P.O. Box 32 - 213 Deer Harbor Road   360-376-2500
Orcas, WA 98280   800-669-3948
Kim Haines   360-376-4453 FAX
E-mail: windsong@pacificrim.net
www.windsonginn.com
Island retreat • 1917 country schoolhouse • Established 1991 with private baths, queen and king beds • Spacious rooms • "Breakfast is King" • Well rated in national automobile and local guide books.

San Juan Island

ARGYLE HOUSE B&B

P.O. Box 2569 - 685 Argyle Avenue   360-378-4084
Friday Harbor, WA 98250
Bill & Chris Carli
Classic 1910 Craftsman home with charm and character • 3 rooms with private baths • Private honeymoon cottage • Hot tub • Delicious full breakfast • Peaceful one acre setting • Walk to town and ferry.

San Juan Island (Con't.)

THE DUFFY HOUSE B&B

4214 Pear Point Road
Friday Harbor, WA 98250
Arthur Miller
E-mail: duffyhouse@rockisland.com
duffyhousebnb.com

360-378-5604
800-972-2089
360-378-6535 FAX

Charming 1920's Tudor-style home • 1-1/2 mi. from town • Overlooking Griffen Bay with beach • Rural setting with orchard and country garden • Five rooms with private baths • Full breakfast • Intoxicatingly quiet.

HIGHLAND INN OF SAN JUAN ISLAND

P.O. Box 135 - 439 Hannah Road
Friday Harbor, WA 98250
Helen C. King
E-mail: helen@highlandinn.com
www.highlandinn.com

360-378-9450
888-400-9850
360-378-1693 FAX

Nestled on wooded hillside • View orca whales, Victoria & Olympic Mountains from 88' veranda • 2 luxury suites, king beds, wood fireplaces, TV, phone, private bath with steam bath and jet tubs for two.

HILLSIDE HOUSE B&B

365 Carter Avenue
Friday Harbor, WA 98250
Dick & Cathy Robinson
E-mail: info@hillsidehouse.com

360-378-4730
800-232-4730
360-378-4715 FAX

Great mountain and water views • Close to town • 7 rooms with privte baths • Honeymoon retreat with spa & fireplace • 2 story atrium • Bicycle shed • Full breakfast • AAA & Mobil • Fodor's • Lanier's.

THE MEADOWS B&B

1557 Cattle Point Road
Friday Harbor, WA 98250
Dodie & Burr Henion
E-mail: dodieburr7@rockisland.com
www.san-juan-island.net/meadows

360-378-4004

Mountain and water views, giant oaks and wild roses • Great beds and good books in 2 spacious guesthouse rooms, each with queen and twin bed • Breakfast in 1892 farmhouse • Enjoy sunroom and deck.

MOON & SIXPENCE

3501 Beaverton Valley Road
Friday Harbor, WA 98250
Evelyn Tuller
E-mail: evtuller@moonandsixpence.net
www.moonandsixpence.net

360-378-4138
888-315-7849

Classic country Bed & Breakfast • Private water tower for two with loft and bath • Family flat for up to 6 with 2 baths • Weaving workshops • Artist's retreat • Continental-plus breakfast • 3 miles to ferry.

San Juan Island (Con't.)

OLYMPIC LIGHTS

146 Starlight Way
Friday Harbor, WA 98250
Christian & Lea Andrade
www.olympiclightsbnb.com

360-378-3186
888-211-6195
360-378-2097 FAX

Magnificent view of the sea and Olympic Mountains from this lovely 1895 Victorian farmhouse on San Juan Island • 4 rooms with private baths • Full breakfast includes eggs from our resident hens • 5-1/2 miles from the ferry.

TOWER HOUSE B&B

392 Little Road
Friday Harbor, WA 98250
Chris & Joe Luma
E-mail: towerhouse@san-juan-island.com
www.san-juan-island.com

360-378-5464
800-858-4276
360-378-5464 FAX

Queen Anne style home on 10 acres overlooking San Juan Valley • 2 rooms, private baths and sitting rooms • Full breakfast with china, crystal, silver and antique linens • Three miles from town.

TRUMPETER INN B&B

318 Trumpeter Way
Friday Harbor, WA 98250
Don & Bobbie Wiesner
E-mail: swan@rockisland.com
trumpeterinn.com

360-378-3884
800-826-7926
360-378-8235 FAX

Pastoral setting with view of water and Olympic Mountains • 5 rooms with private baths • Some with decks and fireplaces • Hot tub • Scrumptious full breakfast • 2 miles from the ferry landing • AAA.

Seabeck

LA CACHETTE B&B

P.O. Box 920 - 10312 Seabeck Hwy.
Seabeck, WA 98380
Chris & Mike Robbins
E-mail: lacachette@moriah.com

360-613-2845
888-613-2845
360-613-2912 FAX

French Country inn on Hood Canal • 4 luxurious suites with private baths • Fireplaces • King size beds • 10 acres of forest and pasture • 2 ponds • A creek • Full breakfast • Lots of amenities.

Seattle

CHELSEA STATION ON THE PARK

4915 Linden Avenue North
Seattle, WA 98103
Eric & Carolanne Watness
E-mail: info@bandbseattle.com
www.bandbseattle.com

206-547-6077
800-400-6077
206-632-5107 FAX

Renew your spirit in our environmentally friendly 1929 inn • Walk to Woodland Park and neighborhood restaurants • Minutes from downtown • Private baths • Hearty breakfasts • Bottomless cookie jar!

ENGLISH TUDOR VIEW

2227 - 72nd Avenue S.E.
Mercer Island, WA 98040
Jo Ann & Bert Schenek
E-mail: tudorview@webtv.net
www.jac1.com

206-232-1373
800-914-5170
206-236-6104 FAX

6 minutes to downtown Seattle from this charming, elegant home • Tastefully decorated • Beautiful view, next to park • Peaceful garden setting • Delicious breakfast • A warm welcome awaits you.

THE GUEST HOUSE B&B

1121 S.W. 160th
Seattle, WA 98166
Tom & Linda Dike
E-mail: guesthse@wolfenet.com
www.wolfenet.com/~guesthse/

206-439-7576
206-439-7576 FAX

Minutes from Seattle-Tacoma Airport and Safeco Field • Tastefully decorated private two bedroom suite • Casual comfort • Warm hospitality • Fireplace • Sundeck with hot tub • Colorful gardens • Delicious breakfast.

SOUNDVIEW B&B

17600 Sylvester Road S.W.
Seattle, WA 98166
Gerry & Dick Flaten
E-mail: soundview@soundviewbandb.com
www.soundviewbandb.com

206-244-5209
888-244-5209
206-243-8687 FAX

Secluded guest house overlooking Puget Sound & Olympic Mountains • King bed • Living room • Kitchen • Private deck with hot tub • TV/VCR/CD • Smoke free • Close to Seattle-Tacoma Airport & downtown • MC/Visa.

VILLA HEIDELBERG

4845 - 45th Avenue S.W.
Seattle, WA 98116
Judith Burbrink
E-mail: info@villaheidelberg.com
www.villaheidelberg.com

206-938-3658
800-671-2942
206-935-7077 FAX

A 1909 Craftsman style home in West Seattle • Leaded glass • Beamed ceilings • Fireplaces • Wraparound porch • Spectacular view • Full breakfast • Included in *Seattle Best Places* • Convenient location.

Sequim

GLENNA'S GUTHRIE COTTAGE B&B

10083 Old Olympic Hwy.   360-681-4349
Sequim, WA 98382   800-930-4349
Jack & Glenna O'Neil   360-681-4349 FAX
E-mail: glenna@olypen.com
www.olypen.com/glennas
Comfortable home in picturesque Sequim-Dungeness Valley • Just minutes from
Highway 101 • Secluded and peaceful • 4 rooms • Some with private bath •
TV/VCR • Soaking tub • Private entrance.

Silverdale

HEAVEN'S EDGE B&B

7410 N.W. Ioka Drive   360-613-1111
Silverdale, WA 98383   800-413-5680
Mary Lee & Don Duley   360-692-4444 FAX
E-mail: marylee@heavensedge.com
www.heavensedge.com
Waterfront estate • Gorgeous views • Private entry • 3-room suite • TV/VCR •
Pampering is our specialty • Gourmet breakfast • Fresh flowers, fruit, cider • Too
many comforts to list! • Smoke free • No pets.

Spokane

ANGELICA'S B&B

1321 West 9th Avenue   509-624-5598
Spokane, WA 99204   800-987-0053
Lynette White-Gustafson   509-624-5598 FAX
E-mail: info@angelicasbb.com
www.angelicasbb.com
Romantic elegance • 1907 Cutter mansion on Historic Registry • Four lovely
bedrooms • Private baths • Fireplace • Sunroom • Full breakfast • Near shopping,
airport, I-90 • Ideal for teas, receptions, small weddings.

THE FOTHERINGHAM HOUSE

2128 West 2nd Avenue   509-838-1891
Spokane, WA 99204   509-838-1807 FAX
Jackie & Graham Johnson
E-mail: innkeeper@fotheringham.net
fotheringham.net
Restoration award-winning 1891 Victorian home of Spokane's first mayor • 4 air-
conditioned rooms • Rose gardens • National Historic District • Near airport, I-90,
golf, park, City Center, Patsy Clark's Restaurant.

Spokane (Con't.)

MARIANNA STOLTZ HOUSE B&B
427 East Indiana Avenue 509-483-4316
Spokane, WA 99207 800-978-6587
Phyllis Maguire 509-483-6773 FAX
E-mail: mstoltz@aimcomm.com
www.mariannastoltzhouse.com
1908 historic inn famous for good food and a friendly atmosphere • Private baths • Cable TV • A/C • Affordable • Near I-90, Gonzaga University and downtown • Nationally rated • Take a virtual walk through our website.

WAVERLY PLACE B&B
709 West Waverly Place 509-328-1856
Spokane, WA 99205 509-326-7059 FAX
Marge & Tammy Arndt
E-mail: waverly@ior.com
www.waverlyplace.com
Delighting guests since 1986 • Award winning restoration of 1902 Victorian • Corbin Park Historic District • Rooms with view of the park • Romantic suite • Air-conditioning • Pool • Full breakfast • *NW Best Places* • Fodor's.

Tacoma

COMMENCEMENT BAY B&B
3312 North Union Avenue 253-752-8175
Tacoma, WA 98407 253-759-4025 FAX
Sharon & Bill Kaufmann
E-mail: greatviews@aol.com
www.great-views.com
Elegant Colonial Inn • Spectacular bay/mountain views • KING-5 TV's "Top Great Washington Escape" • Near shops & waterfront • Hot tub • Private baths • TV/VCR • Phones, dataports • Masseuse • Fantastic breakfasts • Featured in *NW Best Places*.

DEVOE MANSION
208 East 133rd Street 253-539-3991
Tacoma, WA 98445 888-539-3991
Dave & Cheryl Teifke 253-539-8539 FAX
E-mail: innkeeper@devoemansion.com
devoemansion.com
Beautiful 1911 Colonial Mansion on National Historic Register • 4 antique-filled guest rooms • Private baths with soaking tubs • Fireplace • Incredible full breakfast • Gracious hospitality • Come relax • One hour to Seattle.

Tacoma (Con't.)

PALISADES B&B AT DASH POINT

5162 S.W. 311th Place   253-838-4376
Federal Way, WA 98023   888-838-4376
Dennis & Peggy Laporte   253-838-1480 FAX
E-mail: laporte2@ix.netcom.com
palisadesbb.com
Elegant suite • Marbled spa-bath with jacuzzi/double shower • Beautiful room
fireplace • TV/VCR • Very private • Waterfront • Olympic Mountains & Puget
Sound view • 25 minutes south of airport • Full gourmet breakfast.

THE GREEN CAPE COD B&B

2711 North Warner   253-752-1977
Tacoma, WA 98407   253-756-9886 FAX
Mary Beth King
E-mail: grncapecod@aol.com
www.greencapecod.com
1929 Cape Cod in historic University of Puget Sound neighborhood • Cozy rooms
with antiques, private baths, TV's • Fireplace • Full breakfasts • Close to
waterfront restaurants, shops and downtown.

Trout Lake

THE FARM - A B&B

490 Sunnyside Road   509-395-2488
Trout Lake, WA 98650   509-395-2127 FAX
Dean & Rosie Hostetter
E-mail: innkeeper@thefarmbnb.com
www.thefarmbnb.com
Charming 1890 farmhouse • Antiques • Farm breakfast • Mount Adams • Hike •
Bike • Raft • Huckleberry picking • Cross-country ski • Fodor's Guide • National
Geographic Guide To America's Hidden Corners.

Uniontown

THE CHURCHYARD INN

206 St. Boniface Street   509-229-3200
Uniontown, WA 99179   509-229-3213 FAX
Marvin & Linda Entel
E-mail: cyf@inlandnet.com
www.bedandbreakfast.com
A lovely 1905 Victorian Inn and old world setting • Listed on National Historic
Registry • 7 unique rooms with private baths • Handicap accessible bed/bath •
King/Queen/Double/Single beds • Meeting/Luncheon/Weddings/Receptions/Parties
• 16 miles to Pullman • 17 miles to Moscow & Lewiston, ID • 18 miles to
Clarkston, WA.

Vashon Island

ANGELS OF THE SEA B&B

26431 - 99th Avenue S.W.   206-463-6980
Vashon, WA 98070   800-798-9249
Marnie Jones   206-463-2205 FAX
E-mail: AngelsSea@aol.com
www.angelsofthesea.com
Peaceful 1917 country church • Live harp with full breakfast • Suite with private
bath and jacuzzi tub • Two rooms with shared bathroom and guest living room •
Privileges at local country club • KIDS! • Weddings.

OLD TJOMSLAND HOUSE

P.O. Box 913   206-463-5275
17011 Vashon Hwy. S.W.   888-255-2706
Vashon Island, WA 98070   206-463-5275 FAX
Jan & Bill Morosoff
E-mail: jb.morosoff@gateway.net
Take a ferry to the country to Grandma's 1890 farmhouse on beautiful rural island •
2 bedroom suite • 1 bedroom romantic cottage • Privacy • Nurturing comfort •
Farm breakfast • MC/Visa/Discover.

Walla Walla

GREEN GABLES INN

922 Bonsella Street   509-525-5501
Walla Walla, WA 99362   888-525-5501
Jim & Margaret Buchan   509-529-5500 FAX
E-mail: greengables@wwics.com
www.greengablesinn.com
Historic 1909 Craftsman mansion • Rooms have private baths, TV's, refrigerator •
Carriage house cottage suited for families • Located in Whitman College campus
area of stately old homes • Close to town.

Wenatchee

APPLE COUNTRY B&B

524 Okanogan Avenue   509-664-0400
Wenatchee, WA 98801   509-664-6448 FAX
Jerry & Sandi Anderson
E-mail: innkeepers@applecountryinn.com
applecountryinn.com
Charming 1918 home • 4 rooms in main house plus separate carriage house sleeps
4 • Full breakfast served daily • Listed on local Historic Register • TV & hot tub.

WHIDBEY ISLAND - Clinton

SPINK'S OCEAN VIEW

3493 East French Road
Clinton, WA 98236
Lyle & Ann Spink
E-mail: spink@whidbey.com

360-579-2494
888-799-5979
360-579-1970 FAX

2 incredible suites • Veranda • Spacious rooms • Extensive deck • Reunions, receptions, retreats • Accommodates 11, plus babies • Gourmet kitchen • Lawn games • Beach 1 mile • Dormers • Your own hideaway.

THE FARMHOUSE

2740 East Sunshine Lane
Clinton, WA 98236
Janie & Gary Gabelein
E-mail: jon@whidbey.com
www.farmhousebb.com

360-321-6288
888-888-7022

"Come Home to The FARMHOUSE • We have Something Special for You" • Fireplaces • Jacuzzi bath • Kitchens • Private entrances • Mountain & water view • Romantic, spacious suites • In-room breakfast • Homemade Dessert • Hot Tub.

WHIDBEY ISLAND - Langley

EAGLES NEST INN

4680 Saratoga Road
Langley, WA 98260
Jerry & Joanne Lechner
E-mail: eaglnest@whidbey.com

360-221-5331
800-243-5536
360-221-5331 FAX

Hilltop retreat • Panoramic views of Saratoga Passage and Mt. Baker • Superbly appointed suites, each with private bath and deck, TV/VCR/CD • Outdoor spa • Northwest breakfast • Wildlife trails.

THE LOG CASTLE B&B

4693 Saratoga Road
Langley, WA 98260
Jack & Norma Metcalf, Owners
Phil & Karen Holdsworth, Innkeepers
E-mail: innkeepr@thelogcastle.com
www.thelogcastle.com

360-221-5483
360-221-6249 FAX

Inviting, hand-built log lodge on Puget Sound • Stunning water and mountain views in any one of our 4 guest rooms, with private baths • Scrumptious hot breakfasts served at our log table • Canoe • Trails.

Bed & Breakfast Cookbooks from Individual Inns

Heart Healthy Hospitality - Low Fat Breakfast Recipes / The Manor At Taylor's Store
Features 130 low-fat breakfast recipes. Special lay-flat binding. 160 pgs. $10.95

Mountain Mornings - Breakfasts and other recipes from The Inn at 410 B&B
Features 90 tempting recipes. Special lay-flat binding. 128 pgs. $10.95

National & State Association Bed & Breakfast Cookbooks

American Mornings - Favorite Breakfast Recipes From Bed & Breakfast Inns
Features breakfast recipes from 302 inns throughout the country, with complete
information about each inn. 320 pgs. $12.95

What's Cooking Inn Arizona - A Recipe Guidebook of the AZ Assn. of B&B Inns
Features 126 recipes from 21 Arizona inns. 96 pgs. $12.95

Pure Gold - Colorado Treasures / Recipes From B&B Innkeepers of Colorado
Features over 100 recipes from 54 Colorado inns. 96 pgs. $9.95

Colorado Columbine Delicacies - Recipes From B&B Innkeepers of Colorado
Features 115 recipes from 43 Colorado inns. Special lay-flat binding. 112 pgs. $10.95

Inn Good Taste - A Collection of Colorado's Best B&B Recipes
Features 191 recipes from 64 Colorado inns. 176 pgs. $14.95

Inn-describably Delicious - Recipes From The Illinois B&B Assn. Innkeepers
Features recipes from 82 Illinois inns. 112 pgs. $9.95

The Indiana Bed & Breakfast Association Cookbook and Directory
Features recipes from 75 Indiana inns. 96 pgs. $9.95

Hoosier Hospitality - Favorite Recipes from Indiana's Finest B&B Inns
Features over 125 recipes from 54 Indiana inns. 128 pgs. $10.95

Savor the Inns of Kansas - Recipes From Kansas Bed & Breakfasts
Features recipes from 51 Kansas inns. 112 pgs. $9.95

Another Sunrise in Kentucky
Features 110 recipes from 47 Kentucky inns. 112 pgs. $9.95

Sunrise To Sunset in Kentucky
Features over 100 recipes from 48 Kentucky inns. 112 pgs. $12.95

Just Inn Time for Breakfast (Michigan Lake To Lake B&B Association)
Features recipes from 93 Michigan inns. Special lay-flat binding. 128 pgs. $10.95

Be Our Guest - Cooking with Missouri's Innkeepers
Features recipes from 43 Missouri inns. 96 pgs. $9.95

A Taste of Montana
Features 84 recipes from 33 Montana inns. 96 pgs. $10.95

Oklahoma Hospitality Innstyle - A Collection of Oklahoma's Finest B&B Recipes
Features over 117 recipes from 25 Oklahoma inns.   96 pgs. $12.95

Palmetto Hospitality - Inn Style (South Carolina)
Features over 90 recipes from 47 South Carolina inns. 112 pgs. $10.00

South Dakota Sunrise - A Collection of Breakfast Recipes
Features 94 recipes from 37 South Dakota inns. 96 pgs. $10.95

A Taste of Washington State
Features 250 recipes from 83 Washington inns. 192 pgs. $14.95

Another Taste of Washington State
Features 290 recipes from 89 Washington inns. 224 pgs. $15.95

Good Morning West Virginia! - Travel Guide & Recipe Collection
Features 119 recipes from 60 West Virginia inns & travel information. 160 pgs. $12.95

ORDER FORM

To order by phone, please call 800-457-3230.
Visa and MasterCard accepted.

Indicate the quantity of the book(s) that you wish to order below.
Please feel free to copy this form for your order.

MAIL THIS ORDER TO:

Winters Publishing, P.O. Box 501, Greensburg, IN   47240

Quantity

_____	*Heart Healthy Hospitality*	$10.95 each _____
_____	*Mountain Mornings*	$10.95 each _____
_____	*American Mornings*	$12.95 each _____
_____	*What's Cooking Inn Arizona*	$12.95 each _____
_____	*Pure Gold - Colorado Treasures*	$9.95 each _____
_____	*Colorado Columbine Delicacies*	$10.95 each _____
_____	*Inn Good Taste - Colorado*	$14.95 each _____
_____	*Inn-describably Delicious - Illinois*	$9.95 each _____
_____	*Indiana B&B Assn. Cookbook*	$9.95 each _____
_____	*Hoosier Hospitality - Indiana*	$10.95 each _____
_____	*Savor the Inns of Kansas*	$9.95 each _____
_____	*Another Sunrise in Kentucky*	$9.95 each _____
_____	*Sunrise To Sunset in Kentucky*	$12.95 each _____
_____	*Just Inn Time for Breakfast - Michigan*	$10.95 each _____
_____	*Be Our Guest - Missouri*	$9.95 each _____
_____	*A Taste of Montana*	$10.95 each _____
_____	*Oklahoma Hospitality Innstyle*	$12.95 each _____
_____	*Palmetto Hospitality - South Carolina*	$10.00 each _____
_____	*South Dakota Sunrise*	$10.95 each _____
_____	*A Taste of Washington State*	$14.95 each _____
_____	*Another Taste of Washington State*	$15.95 each _____
_____	*Good Morning West Virginia!*	$12.95 each _____

Shipping Charge $2.00 1st book, $1.00 each additional.   _____

5% Sales Tax (IN residents <u>ONLY</u>)   _____

TOTAL   _____

Send to:

Name: _____

Address: _____

City: _____ State: _____ Zip: _____

Phone: (_____) _____